DATE			

warren shibles, comp.
University of Wisconsin - Whitewater

ESSAYS ON
METAPHOR

THE LANGUAGE PRESS

Box 342 Whitewater, Wisconsin 53190

By the same author:

Metaphor: An Annotated Bibliography and History Whitewater, Wisc.: The Language Press 1971.

Philosophical Pictures Dubuque, Iowa: Kendall-Hunt 1969 (revised 1972)

Wittgenstein, Language and Philosophy Kendall-Hunt 1969 (1971)

Models of Ancient Greek Philosophy London: Vision Press (New York: Humanities) 1971

An Analysis of Metaphor The Hague: Mouton (New York: Humanities) 1971

Emotions: A Conceptual Analysis Feb. 1973 The Language Press

Death: A Conceptual Analysis Feb. 1973 The Language Press

Printed in the United States of America

"The greatest thing by far is to be a master of metaphor."

Aristotle

"Metaphor has always been one of the central problems of philosophy."

D. Berggren

"Whole works of scientific research, even entire schools, are hardly more than the patient repetition, in all its ramifications, of a fertile metaphor."

Kenneth Burke

"Both philosophers and poets live by metaphor."

S. Pepper

"A philosophical treatise has never been written which did not depend upon the use of metaphor."

D. Berggren

"The most fruitful modern criticism is a rediscovery and recovery of the importance of metaphor."

C. Brooks

"Any history of thought might begin and end with the statement that man is an analogical animal."

S. Buchanan

"Metaphor was the beginning of wisdom, the earliest scientific method."

C. Day-Lewis

"To know is to use metaphor."   M. Friquegnon

"All thinking is metaphorical."   Robert Frost

"The most profound social creativity consists in the invention and imposition of new, radical metaphors."

R. Kaufmann

"All our truth, or all but a few fragments, is won by metaphor."

C. S. Lewis

"And what therefore is truth? A mobile army of metaphors. . . . Truths are illusions of which one has forgotten that they are illusions."

Nietzsche

"To know is merely to work with one's favorite metaphors."

Nietzsche

"I recommend a microscopic venture, concerned with tracing fine distinctions according to the imagery appropriate to each art form."

M. Osborn

"Any supreme insight is a metaphor."

H. Parkhurst

"Poets, it is said, anticipate science . . . . The finest instrument of these discoveries is metaphor. . ."

Sir Walter Raleigh

"What is not verbally odd is devoid of disclosure power."

I. Ramsey

"A better understanding of metaphor is one of the aims which an improved curriculum of literary studies might well set before itself."

I. A. Richards

"As philosophy grows more abstract we think increasingly by means of metaphors that we profess *not* to be relying on."

I. A. Richards

"The conduct of even the plainest, most 'direct' untechnical prose is a ceaseless exercise in metaphor."

I. A. Richards

"Language is vitally metaphorical." Shelley

"Every great breakthrough in science, every scientific revolution, has also been a poetic revolution because it has created a new paradigm of thought."

Warren Bennis

Table of Contents

Introduction

I On Truth and Falsity in their Extramoral Sense
by Friedrich Nietzsche 1

II The Root Metaphor Theory of Metaphysics
by Stephen C. Pepper 15

III Metaphor
by John Middleton Murry 27

IV Imagery: From Sensation to Symbol
by Norman Friedman 41

V Semantics and Ontology
by Philip Wheelwright 61

VI The Metaphorical Twist
by Monroe C. Beardsley 73

VII Pictorial Meaning, Picture Thinking, and Wittgenstein's
Theory of Aspects
by Virgil Aldrich 93

VIII Art and the Human Form
by Virgil Aldrich 105

IX Metaphor and Aspect Seeing
by Marcus B. Hester 111

X Anxiety: Reification of a Metaphor
by Theodore R. Sarbin 125

XI Synectics
by Eugene Raudsepp 141

XII Visual/Verbal Rhetoric
by Gui Bonsiepe 155

XIII Models and Mystery
by Ian T. Ramsey 163

XIV Scientific Models
by Mary Hesse 169

Preface

This is the first collection of essays on metaphor, the concept which is said to be the central method of science, poetry, literature, philosophy, language, psychology, psychiatry, etc. These essays were selected from about three thousand essays, books, dissertations, etc. appearing in my previous work, *Metaphor: An Annotated Bibliography and History*.[1] They attempt to clarify the notion of metaphor from the perspectives of philosophy, literature and literary criticism, poetry, psychology, linguistics, religion, philosophy of science, synectics or creative development in industry, and advertising. The book is intended to help clarify and promote research on the concept of metaphor. Its ultimate aim is to promote inquiry and conceptual clarification.

1. W. Shibles *Metaphor: An Annotated Bibliography and History* Whitewater, Wisconsin: The Language Press 1971. See also W. Shibles *An Analysis of Metaphor* The Hague: Mouton (New York: Humanities Press) 1971. Both volumes contain an extensive analytical index of ideas about metaphor.

Introduction

I Brief Summary of the Essays

According to Nietzsche, by metaphor we translate from sense perception to image, from image to language, from nerve stimulus to percept to sound. We metaphorically divide things up into genders. Language is fundamentally metaphorical and man has a basic drive to create them, though he is not usually aware that he uses them. Truths are merely metaphors which we forgot are metaphors. Truths are illusions, not things in themselves. The intentional adherence to illusion in spite of our awareness of it is a kind of "lie in an extra-moral sense."

In Pepper's article metaphor is presented as a method or basis of philosophy. The "root-metaphor" is a small concept or hypothesis applied to a larger range of events. We usually think in such metaphors. But no single metaphor is adequate. Several are needed. He opposes dogmatic philosophies which are unaware of their root metaphors. Root metaphors have their own logic and are not bound by universal principles, e.g., principle of non-contradiction. In his book, *World Hypothesis,*[1] he shows how metaphor generates the four main philosophical theories, or world views are generated from the root metaphors 1) formism 2) mechanism 3) contextualism 4) organicism.

Murry's article is from the literary perspective. For him metaphor is inextricably bound up with language and thought. It is basic to thought, knowledge and insight. In fact, inquiry into metaphor presupposes a metaphorical method of inquiry. He writes, "We find ourselves questioning the very faculty and instrument with which we are trying to penetrate them."

Friedman provides a summary and analysis of the various views of metaphor or imagery from the literary perspective.

Wheelwright, a philosopher and literary critic, discusses metaphor from the perspective of language. He distinguishes between "epiphor," an antecedent resemblance or implicit analogy justifying the metaphor, and "diaphor," an induced resemblance. Diaphor is novel, untranslatable, paradoxical and irreducible. Both types of metaphor partially constitute real objects. "Block" or "steno" language of science is distinguished from more adequate, metaphorical, tensive language.

Beardsley presents a philosophical analysis of metaphor. According to his "Revised Verbal-Opposition View[2] the two terms of a metaphor if taken literally yield absurdity. Thus there is a "twist" to connotative meaning in which the predicate gains a new intension. The revision involves including larger contextual considerations.

In "Pictorial Meaning . . .", Aldrich discusses Ludwig Wittgenstein's notion of "seeing-as" or "aspect-seeing." Aldrich modifies this view to include in it an aesthetic image-exhibiting or picturing function of language rather than just meaning as use. His most recent statement in "Art and the Human Form" expands on this view in terms of what may be called "visual metaphor." He calls his new theory the "function theory of metaphor." It stresses the presentational immediacy of metaphorical perception.

Hester also accepts much of Wittgenstein's theory of meaning and also goes beyond this view by asserting that metaphors involve imagery. He stresses "reading" as an act of seeing-as by which the relevant sense of a metaphor is found. The read metaphor has presentational immediacy.

The psychologist Sarbin states that the mentalistic term, anxiety, and Freud's metaphors are based on myth which arises when one takes one's metaphors literally. It is a metaphor-to-myth fallacy. Anxiety is not an internal or mental state, not a thing, and so not a thing to be purged of. He offers an alternative and admittedly metaphorical account.

Raudsepp presents an account of Synectics,[3] a method of solving problems in business and industry as well as in other areas. Synectics, Inc. is a corporation in Cambridge, Mass., established for this purpose. What mainly characterizes this method is its reliance on metaphor. Although its promoters have presented it as being based on Freudian psychology, I believe that its basis is rather in the logic of the concept and use of metaphor. Metaphor promotes "free association."

Gui Bonsiepe, Editor of *The Journal of the Ulm School of Design,* presents a modern system of rhetoric based on syntactic and semantic distinctions involving the visual as well as the verbal in applying rhetoric to advertising.

Ramsey applies his views of metaphor to religion and science. For him metaphors and models give a unique insight into reality. In a metaphor two ideas cooperate in an inclusive meaning-giving "mystery" generating an insight or "disclosure" which is geared to the context of that insight and arises out of it. He writes, "What is not verbally odd is devoid of disclosure power."

From the perspective of the philosophy of science, Hesse writes that analogies or metaphoric models in science may not just illustrate but rather determine the phenomena. They often cannot be reduced to similes or rendered in more precise terms without destroying their heuristic value. The use of mathematics in describing nature is always merely analogical.

II

The various ideas and sorts of statements which have been made about metaphor have been analytically indexed in a 95-page index in *Metaphor: An Annotated Bibliography and History*.[4] These topics may serve to characterize the nature of metaphor more adequately than could possibly be done here. Several such topics are Metaphor: to describe abstract by concrete, in actions, anagogic, as analogical, as antithesis, archetypal, artificial, as as-if, as basis of arts and sciences, as behavioral, being captivated by, as catachresis, as catharsis, classification of, as cliche, as collage, as comparison, as concealing, as concise, as concrete, in context, controversion theory of, and counterfactuals, in creativity, crisis, as representing a culture or age, in cursing, dead, as defense mechanism, as delusion, as description, as deviation, diagrams of, as dialectic, as disclosure, as dissolving distinctions, as distance, distrust of, in drama, as drawn or sketched, and drugs, in education, as ellipsis, as emblem, as constituting emotions, as descriptive of emotions, as expressing emotions, as stimulating emotions, as emotive, empathetic, as epic or historical form, as escape, as ethical term, as basis of etymology, as euphemism, excess of, exercises in, expansion of, as experience, as expressing the inexpressible, as expressive, as fable, false, familiar, as fantasy, far-fetched, as fiction, in film, as filter, fixed, as formula, Freudian theories of, fundamental, as fusion, in games, of gender, genitive link, as a work of genius, based on genus-species transference, good, grammatical, as harmony, hidden, as honest, as humanizing, as humor, as hyperbole, as hypothesis, as expressing ideas, as identity, as illogical, as illustrating, as image, as product of imagination and fancy, based on imagined relation, as rendering immaterial by material, as immediate experience, indirect, as inexhaustible concept, representation of inner by outer, as giving insight, as intellectual, intentional, as interaction, as intuited, as irrational, as juxtaposition, as kenning, as source of knowledge, to express unknown by known, as likeness, as not based on likeness, linguistic theory of, as indistinguishable from literal, as irreducible to literal, as reducible to literal statement, taken literally, mediational processes of, as metamorphosis, of metaphor, built on metaphors, as metaphysics, as metonymy, to describe mind, misuse of, mixed, as model, as montage, and multiple meanings, in music, as mystical (miraculous, wonder, mystery, marvelous, anagogical, transcendent, visions), as myth, as a naming, as natural, as necessary principle of language development, negative, as new, as nonsense, of omitting, in oratory, origin of, as ornamenting, in painting, as a parable, as paradigm, as paradox, parallelism, as parataxis, perceptual, as descriptive of persons, as perspective, as persuasive, as basis of a philosophy, in philosophy, based on physiological states, as pictorial, plastic, as play, as pleasing, poetic, in political science, as possible explanation, as presentational, as pretending, as primitive, psychological or psychiatric theory of, as puzzle, as having a common quality, in reading, as constituting reality, to describe reality, reciprocal, rejuvenated, as relation, as repetition, as governed by rules, in schizophrenia, in science, as seeing-as, as a sentence, of silence, as simile, sinking, as slang, influence on speaker, as representing spiritual by sensual, as the sublime, as a substitution, as suggestive, as surprise, symbolic, synaesthetic, as synecdoche, as synthesis, as based on taboo, as tension, as a single term, test for, as therapy, as constituting thought, in thought, as transfer, as true, as type-crossing, as unifying, as unity in difference, as attempt to reach universals, in value, non-verbal, verification of, as rendering the invisible by the visible, visual.

These characteristics provide a general idea as to the nature of metaphor and may serve as a guide in organizing and thinking about points made in the following essays. It allows the reader to put such ideas in context. As nearly every article here has already been analytically indexed in the above mentioned annotated metaphor bibliography no attempt is made to do so again here.

1. Stephen Pepper *World Hypothesis* Berkeley: University of California Press 1942.

2. The unrevised version is in M. C. Beardsley *Aesthetics* New York: Harcourt, Brace and World, 1958, pp. 133-147, 159-162.

3. See also William Gordon *Synectics,* New York: Harper and Row, 1961.

4. W. Shibles, *op. cit.*

On Truth and Falsity in their Extramoral Sense

Friedrich Nietzsche

In some remote corner of the universe, effused into innumerable solar-systems, there was once a star upon which clever animals invented cognition. It was the haughtiest, most mendacious moment in the history of this world, but yet only a moment. After Nature had taken breath awhile the star congealed and the clever animals had to die. — Someone might write a fable after this style, and yet he would not have illustrated sufficiently, how wretched, shadow-like, transitory, purposeless and fanciful the human intellect appears in Nature. There were eternities during which this intellect did not exist, and when it has once more passed away there will be nothing to show that it has existed. For this intellect is not concerned with any further mission transcending the sphere of human life. No, it is purely human and none but its owner and procreator regards it so pathetically as to suppose that the world revolves around it. If, however, we and the gnat could understand each other we should learn that even the gnat swims through the air with the same pathos, and feels within itself the flying centre of the world. Nothing in Nature is so bad or so insignificant that it will not, at the smallest puff of that force cognition, immediately swell up like a balloon, and just as a mere porter wants to have his admirer, so the very proudest man, the philosopher, imagines he sees from all sides the eyes of the universe telescopically directed upon his actions and thoughts.

It is remarkable that this is accomplished by the intellect, which after all has been given to the most unfortunate, the most delicate, the most transient beings only as an expedient, in order to detain them for a moment in existence, from which without that extra-gift they would have every cause to flee as swiftly as Lessing's son.[2] That haughtiness connected with cognition and sensation, spreading blinding fogs before the eyes and over the senses of men, deceives itself therefore as to the value of existence owing to the fact that it bears within itself the most flattering evaluation of cognition. Its most general effect is deception; but even its most particular effects have something of deception in their nature.

The intellect, as a means for the preservation of the individual, develops its chief power in dissimulation; for it is by dissimulation that the feebler, and less robust individuals preserve themselves, since it has been denied them to fight the battle of existence with horns or the sharp teeth of beasts of prey. In man this art of dissimulation reaches its acme of perfection: in him deception, flattery, falsehood and fraud, slander, display, pretentiousness, disguise, cloaking convention, and acting to others and to himself in short, the continual fluttering to and fro around the *one* flame — Vanity: all these things are so much the rule, and the law, that few things are more incomprehensible than the way in which an honest and pure impulse to truth could have arisen among men. They are deeply immersed in illusions and dream-fancies; their eyes glance only over the surface of things and see "forms"; their sensation nowhere leads to truth, but contents itself with receiving stimuli and, so to say, with playing hide-and-seek on the back of things. In addition to that, at night man allows his dreams to lie to him a whole life-time long, without his moral sense ever trying to prevent them; whereas men are said to exist who by the exercise of a strong will have overcome the habit of snoring. What indeed *does* man know about himself? Oh! that he could but once see himself complete, placed as it were in an illuminated glass-case! Does not nature keep secret from him most things, even about his body, *e.g.,* the convolutions of the intestines, the quick flow of the blood-currents, the intricate vibrations of the fibres, so as to banish and lock him up in proud, delusive knowledge? Nature threw away the key; and woe to the fateful curiosity which might be able for a moment to look out and down through a crevice in the chamber of consciousness, and discover that man, indifferent to his own ignorance, is resting on the pitiless, the greedy, the insatiable, the murderous, and, as it were, hanging in dreams on the back of a tiger. Whence, in the wide world, with this state of affairs, arises the impulse to truth?

As far as the individual tries to preserve himself against other individuals, in the natural state of things he uses the intellect in most cases only for dissimulation; since, however, man both from necessity and boredom wants to exist socially and gregariously, he must needs make peace and at least endeavour to cause the greatest *bellum omnium contra omnes* to disappear from his world. This first conclusion of peace brings with it a something which looks like the first step towards the attainment of that enigmatical bent for truth. For that which henceforth is to be "truth" is now fixed; that is to say, a uniformly valid and binding designation of things is invented and the legislature of language also gives the first laws of truth: since here, for the first time, originates the contrast between truth and falsity. The liar uses the valid designations, the words, in order to make the unreal appear as real; *e.g.,* he says, "I am rich," whereas the right designation for his state would be "poor." He abuses the fixed conventions by convenient substitution or even inversion of terms. If he does this in a selfish and moreover harmful fashion, society will no longer trust him but will even exclude him. In this way men avoid not so much being defrauded, but being injured by fraud. At bottom, at this juncture too, they hate not deception, but the evil, hostile consequences of certain species of deception. And it is in a similarly limited sense only that man desires truth: he covets the agreeable, life-preserving consequences of truth; he is indifferent towards pure, ineffective knowledge; he is even inimical towards truths which possibly might prove harmful or destroying. And, moreover, what after all are those conventions of language? Are they possibly products of knowledge, of the love of truth; do the designations and the things coincide? Is language the adequate expression of all realities?

Only by means of forgetfulness can man ever arrive at imagining that he possesses "truth" in that degree just indicated. If he does not mean to content himself with truth in the shape of tautology, that is, with empty husks, he will always obtain illusions instead of truth. What is a word? The expression of a nerve-stimulus in sounds. But to infer a cause outside us from the nerve-stimulus is already the result of a wrong and unjustifiable application of the proposition of causality. How should we dare, if truth with the genesis of language, if the point of view of certainty with the designations had alone been decisive; how indeed should we dare to say: the stone is hard; as if "hard" was known to us otherwise; and not merely as an entirely subjective stimulus! We divide things according to genders; we designate the tree as masculine,[3] the plant as feminine:[4] what arbitrary metaphors! How far flown beyond the canon of certainty! We speak of a "serpent";[5] the designation fits nothing but the sinuosity, and could therefore also appertain to the worm. What arbitrary demarcations! what one-sided preferences given sometimes to this, sometimes to that quality of a thing! The different languages placed side by side show that with words truth or adequate expression matters little: for otherwise there would not be so many languages. The "Thing-in-itself" (it is just this which would be the pure ineffective truth) is also quite incomprehensible to the creator of language and not worth making any great endeavour to obtain. He designates only the relations of things to men and for their expression he calls to his help the most daring metaphors. A nerve-stimulus, first transformed into a percept! First metaphor! The percept again copied into a sound! Second metaphor! And each time he leaps completely out of one sphere right into the midst of an entirely different one. One can imagine a man who is quite deaf and has never had a sensation of tone and of music; just as this man will possibly marvel at Chladni's sound figures in the sand, will discover their cause in the vibrations of the string, and will then proclaim that now he knows what man calls "tone"; even so does it happen to us all with language. When we talk about trees, colours, snow and flowers, we believe we know something about the things themselves, and yet we only possess metaphors of the things, and these metaphors do not in the least correspond to the original essentials. Just as the sound shows itself as a sand-figure, in the same way the enigmatical x of the Thing-in-itself is seen first as nerve-stimulus, then as percept, and finally as sound. At any rate the genesis of language did not therefore proceed on logical lines, and the whole material in which and with which the man of truth, the investigator, the philosopher works and builds, originates, if not from Nephelococcygia, cloud-land, at any rate not from the essence of things.

Let us especially think about the formation of ideas. Every word becomes at once an idea not by having, as one might presume, to serve as a reminder for the original experience happening but once and absolutely individualized, to which experience such word owes its origin, no, but by having simultaneously to fit innumerable, more or less similar (which really means never equal, therefore altogether unequal) cases. Every idea originates through equating the unequal. As certainly as no one leaf is exactly similar to any other, so certain is it that the idea "leaf" has been formed through an arbitrary omission of these individual differences, through a forgetting of the differentiating qualities, and this idea now awakens the notion that in nature there is, besides the leaves, a something called *the* "leaf," perhaps a primal form according to which all leaves were woven, drawn, accurately measured, coloured, crinkled, painted, but by unskilled hands, so that no copy had turned out correct and trustworthy as a true copy of the primal form. We call a man "honest"; we ask, why has he acted so honestly to-day? Our customary answer runs, "On account of his honesty." *The* Honesty! That means again: the "leaf" is the cause of the leaves. We really and truly do not know anything at all about an essential quality which might be called *the* honesty, but we do know about numerous individualised, and therefore unequal actions, which we equate by omission of the unequal, and now designate as honest actions; finally out of them we formulate a *qualitas occulta* with the name "Honesty." The disregarding of the individual and real furnishes us with the idea, as it likewise also gives us the form; whereas nature knows of no forms and ideas, and therefore knows no species but only an *x,* to us inaccessible and indefinable. For our antithesis of individual and species is anthropomorphic too and does not come from the essence of things, although on the other hand we do not dare to say that it does not correspond to it; for that would be a dogmatic assertion and as such just as undemonstrable as its contrary.

What therefore is truth? A mobile army of metaphors, metonymies, anthropomorphisms: in short a sum of human relations which became poetically and rhetorically intensified, metamorphosed, adorned, and after long usage seem to a nation fixed, canonic and binding; truths are illusions of which one has forgotten that they *are* illusions; worn-out metaphors which have become powerless to affect the senses; coins which have their obverse effaced and now are no longer of account as coins but merely as metal.

Still we do not yet know whence the impulse to truth comes, for up to now we have heard only about the obligation which society imposes in order to exist: to be truthful, that is, to use the usual metaphors, therefore expressed morally: we have heard only about the obligation to lie according to a fixed convention, to lie gregariously in a style binding for all. Now man of course forgets that matters are going thus with him; he therefore lies in that fashion pointed out unconsciously and according to habits of centuries' standing — and by *this very unconsciousness,* by this very forgetting, he arrives at a sense for truth. Through this feeling of being obliged to designate one thing as "red," another as "cold," a third one as "dumb," awakes a moral emotion relating to truth. Out of the antithesis "liar" whom nobody trusts, whom all exclude, man demonstrates to himself the venerableness, reliability, usefulness of truth. Now as a *"rational"* being he submits his actions to the sway of abstractions; he no longer suffers himself to be carried away by sudden impressions, by sensations, he first generalises all these impressions into paler cooler ideas, in order to attach to them the ship of his life and actions. Everything which makes man stand out in bold relief against the animal depends on this faculty of volatilising the concrete metaphors into a schema, and therefore resolving a perception into an idea. For within the range of those schemata a something becomes possible that never could succeed under the first perceptual impressions: to build up a pyramidal order with castes and grades, to create a new world of laws, privileges, sub-orders, delimitations, which now stands opposite the other perceptual world of first impressions and assumes the appearance of being the more fixed, general, known, human of the two and therefore the regulating and imperative one. Whereas every metaphor of perception is individual and without its equal and therefore knows how to escape all attempts to classify it, the great edifice of ideas show the rigid regularity of a Roman Columbarium and in logic breathes forth the sternness and coolness which we find in mathematics. He who has been breathed upon by this coolness will scarcely believe, that the idea too, bony and hexahedral, and permutable as a die, remains however only as the *residuum of a metaphor,* and that the illusion of the artistic metamorphosis of a nerve-stimulus into percepts is, if not the mother, then the grandmother of every idea. Now in this game of dice, "Truth" means to use every die as it is designated, to count its points carefully, to form exact classifications, and never to violate the order of castes and the sequences of rank. Just as the Romans and Etruscans for their benefit cut up the sky by means of strong mathematical lines and banned a god as it were into a *templum,* into a space limited in this fashion, so every nation has above its head such a sky of ideas divided up mathematically, and it understands the demand for truth to mean that every conceptual god is to be looked for only in *his* own sphere. One may here well admire man, who succeeded in piling up an infinitely complex dome of ideas on a movable foundation and as it were on running water, as a powerful genius of architecture. Of course in order to obtain hold on such a foundation it must be as an edifice piled up out of cobwebs, so fragile, as to be carried away by the waves: so firm, as not to be blown asunder by every wind. In this way man as an architectural genius rises high above the bee; she builds with wax, which she brings together out of nature; he with the much more delicate material of ideas, which he must first manufacture within himself. He is very much to be admired here — but not on account of his impulse for truth, his bent for pure cognition of things. If somebody hides a thing behind a bush, seeks it again and finds it in the self-same place, then there is not much to boast of, respecting this seeking and finding; thus, however, matters stand with the seeking and finding of "truth" within the realm of reason. If I make the definition of the mammal and then declare after inspecting a camel, "Behold a mammal," then no doubt a truth is brought to light thereby, but it is of very limited value, I mean it is anthropomorphic through and through, and does not contain one single point which is "true-in-itself," real and universally valid, apart from man. The seeker after such truths seeks at the bottom only the metamorphosis of the world in man, he strives for an understanding of the world as a human-like thing and by his battling gains at best the feeling of an assimilation. Similarly, as the astrologer contemplated the stars in the service of man and in connection with their happiness and unhappiness, such a seeker contemplates the whole world as related to man, as the infinitely protracted echo of an original sound: man; as the multiplied copy of the one arch-type: man. His procedure is to apply man as the measure of all things, whereby he starts from the error of believing that he has these things immediately before him as pure objects. He therefore forgets that the original metaphors of perception *are* metaphors, and takes them for the things themselves.

Only by forgetting that primitive world of metaphors, only by the congelation and coagulation of an original mass of similes and percepts pouring forth as a fiery liquid out of the primal faculty of human fancy, only by the invincible faith, that *this* sun, *this* window, *this* table is a truth in itself: in short only by the fact that man forgets himself as subject, and what is more as an *artistically creating* subject: only by all this does he live with some repose, safety and consequence. If he were able to get out of the prison walls of this faith, even for an instant only, his "self-consciousness" would be destroyed at once. Already it costs him some trouble to admit to himself that the insect and the bird perceive a world different from his own, and that the question, which of the two world-perceptions is more accurate, is quite a senseless one, since to decide this question it would be necessary to apply the standard of *right perception,* i.e., to apply a standard which *does not exist.* On the whole it seems to me that the "right perception" — which would mean the adequate expression of an object in the subject — is a nonentity full of contradictions: for between two utterly different spheres, as between subject and object, there is no causality, no accuracy, no expression, but at the utmost an *aesthetical* relation, I mean a suggestive metamorphosis, a stammering translation into quite a distinct foreign language, for which purpose however there is needed at any rate an intermediate sphere, an intermediate force, freely composing and freely inventing. The word "phenomenon" contains many seductions, and on that account I avoid it as much as possible, for it is not true that the essence of things appears in the empiric world. A painter who had no hands and wanted to express the picture distinctly present to his mind by the agency of song, would still reveal much more with this permutation of spheres, than the empiric world reveals about the essence of things. The very relations of a nerve-stimulus to the produced percept is in itself no necessary one; but if the same percept has been reproduced millions of times and has been the inheritance of many successive generations of man, and in the end appears each time to all mankind as the result of the same cause, then it attains finally for man the same importance as if it were *the* unique, necessary percept and as if that relation between the original nerve-stimulus and the percept produced were a close relation of causality: just as a dream eternally repeated, would be perceived and judged as though real. But the congelation and coagulation of a metaphor does not at all guarantee the necessity and exclusive justification of that metaphor.

Surely every human being who is at home with such contemplations has felt a deep distrust against any idealism of that kind, as often as he has distinctly convinced himself of the eternal rigidity, omni-presence, and infallibility of nature's laws: he has arrived at the conclusion that as far as we can penetrate the heights of the telescopic and the depths of the microscopic world, everything is quite secure, complete, infinite, determined, and continuous. Science will have to dig in these shafts eternally and successfully and all things found are sure to have to harmonize and not to contradict one another. How little does this resemble a product of fancy, for if it were one it would necessarily betray somewhere its nature of appearance and unreality. Against this it may be objected in the first place that if each of us had for himself a different sensibility, if we ourselves were only able to perceive sometimes as a bird, sometimes as a worm, sometimes as a plant, or if one of us saw the same stimulus as red, another as blue, if a third person even perceived it as a tone, then nobody would talk of such an orderliness of nature, but would conceive of her only as an extremely subjective structure. Secondly, what is, for us in general, a law of nature? It is not known in itself but only in its effects, that is to say in its relations to other laws of nature, which again are known to us only as sums of relations. Therefore all these relations refer only one to another and are absolutely incomprehensible to us in their essence; only that which we add: time, space, *i.e.,* relations of sequence and numbers, are really known to us in them. Everything wonderful however, that we marvel at in the laws of nature, everything that demands an explanation and might seduce us into distrusting idealism, lies really and solely in the mathematical rigour and inviolability of the conceptions of time and space. These however we produce within ourselves and throw them forth with that necessity with which the spider spins; since we are compelled to conceive all things under these forms only, then it is no longer wonderful that in all things we actually conceive none but these forms: for they all must bear within themselves the laws of number, and this very idea of number is the most marvellous in all things. All obedience to law which impresses us so forcibly in the orbits of stars and in chemical processes coincides at the bottom with those qualities which we ourselves attach to those things, so that it is we who thereby make the impression upon ourselves. Whence it clearly follows that that artistic formation of metaphors, with which every sensation in us begins, already presupposes those forms, and is therefore only consummated within them; only out of the persistency of these primal forms the possibility explains itself, how afterwards out of the metaphors themselves a structure of ideas could again be compiled. For the latter is an imitation of the relations of time, space and number in the realm of metaphors.

2

As we saw, it is *language* which has worked originally at the construction of ideas; in later times it is *science*. Just as the bee works at the same time at the cells and fills them with honey, thus science works irresistibly at that great columbarium of ideas, the cemetery of perceptions, builds ever newer and higher storeys; supports, purifies, renews the old cells, and endeavours above all to fill that gigantic framework and to arrange within it the whole of the empiric world, *i.e.*, the anthropomorphic world. And as the man of action binds his life to reason and its ideas, in order to avoid being swept away and losing himself, so the seeker after truth builds his hut close to the towering edifice of science in order to collaborate with it and to find protection. And he needs protection. For there are awful powers which continually press upon him, and which hold out against the "truth" of science "truths" fashioned in quite another way, bearing devices of the most heterogeneous character.

That impulse towards the formation of metaphors, that fundamental impulse of man, which we cannot reason away for one moment — for thereby we should reason away man himself — is in truth not defeated nor even subdued by the fact that out of its evaporated products, the ideas, a regular and rigid new world has been built as a stronghold for it. This impulse seeks for itself a new realm of action and another river-bed, and finds it in *Mythos* and more generally in *Art*. This impulse constantly confuses the rubrics and cells of the ideas, by putting up new figures of speech, metaphors, metonymies; it constantly shows its passionate longing for shaping the existing world of waking man as motley, irregular, inconsequentially incoherent, attractive, and eternally new as the world of dreams is. For indeed, waking man *per se* is only clear about his being awake through the rigid and orderly woof of ideas, and it is for this very reason that he sometimes comes to believe that he was dreaming when that woof of ideas has for a moment been torn by Art. Pascal is quite right, when he asserts, that if the same dream came to us every night we should be just as much occupied by it as by the things which we see every day; to quote his words, "If an artisan were certain that he would dream every night for fully twelve hours that he was a king, I believe that he would be just as happy as a king who dreams every night for twelve hours that he is an artisan." The wide-awake day of a people mystically excitable, let us say of the earlier Greeks, is in fact through the continually-working wonder, which the mythos presupposes, more akin to the dream than to the day of the thinker sobered by science. If every tree may at some time talk as a nymph, or a god under the disguise of a bull, carry away virgins, if the goddess Athene herself be suddenly seen as, with a beautiful team, she drives, accompanied by Pisistratus, through the markets of Athens — and every honest Athenian did believe this — at any moment, as in a dream, everything is possible; and all nature swarms around man as if she were nothing but the masquerade of the gods, who found it a huge joke to deceive man by assuming all possible forms.

Man himself, however, has an invincible tendency to let himself be deceived, and he is like one enchanted with happiness when the rhapsodist narrates to him epic romances in such a way that they appear real or when the actor on the stage makes the king appear more kingly than reality shows him. Intellect, that master of dissimulation, is free and dismissed from his service as slave, so long as It is able to deceive without *injuring* and the It celebrates Its Saturnalia. Never is It richer, prouder, more luxuriant, more skilful and daring; with a creator's delight It throws metaphors into confusion, shifts the boundary-stones of the abstractions, so that for instance It designates the stream as the mobile way which carries man to that place whither he would otherwise go. Now It has thrown off Its shoulders the emblem of servitude. Usually with gloomy officiousness It endeavours to point out the way to a poor individual coveting existence, and It fares forth for plunder and booty like a servant for his master, but now It Itself has become a master and may wipe from Its countenance the expression of indigence. Whatever It now does, compared with Its former doings, bears within itself dissimulation, just as Its former doings bore the character of distortion. It copies human life, but takes it for a good thing and seems to rest quite satisfied with it. That enormous framework and hoarding of ideas, by clinging to which needy man saves himself through life, is to the freed intellect only a scaffolding and a toy for Its most daring feats, and when It smashes it to pieces, throws it into confusion, and then puts it together ironically, pairing the strangest, separating the nearest items, then It manifests that It has no use for those makeshifts of misery, and that It is now no longer led by ideas but by intuitions. From these intuitions no regular road leads into the land of the spectral schemata, the abstractions; for them the word is not made, when man sees them he is dumb, or speaks in forbidden metaphors and in unheard-of combinations of ideas, in order to correspond creatively with the impression of the powerful present intuition at least by destroying and jeering at the old barriers of ideas.

There are ages, when the rational and the intuitive man stand side by side, the one full of fear of the intuition, the other full of scorn for the abstraction; the latter just as irrational as the former is inartistic. Both desire to rule over life; the one by knowing how to meet the most important needs with foresight, prudence, regularity; the other as an "over-joyous" hero by ignoring those needs and taking that life only as real which simulates appearance and beauty. Wherever intuitive man, as for instance in the earlier history of Greece, brandishes his weapons more powerfully and victoriously than his opponent, there under favourable conditions, a culture can develop and art can establish her rule over life. That dissembling, that denying of neediness, that splendour of metaphorical notions and especially that directness of dissimulation accompany all utterances of such a life. Neither the house of man, nor his way of walking, nor his clothing, nor his earthen jug suggest that necessity invented them; it seems as if they all were intended as the expressions of a sublime happiness, an Olympic cloudlessness, and as it were a playing at seriousness. Whereas the man guided by ideas and abstractions only wards off misfortune by means of them, without even enforcing for himself happiness out of the abstractions; whereas he strives after the greatest possible freedom from pains, the intuitive man dwelling in the midst of culture has from his intuitions a harvest: besides the warding off of evil, he attains a continuous in-pouring of enlightenment, enlivenment and redemption. Of course when he *does* suffer, he suffers more: and he even suffers more frequently since he cannot learn from experience, but again and again falls into the same ditch into which he has fallen before. In suffering he is just as irrational as in happiness; he cries aloud and finds no consolation. How different matters are in the same misfortune with the Stoic, taught by experience and ruling himself by ideas! He who otherwise only looks for uprightness, truth, freedom from deceptions and shelter from ensnaring and sudden attack, in his misfortune performs the masterpiece of dissimulation, just as the other did in his happiness; he shows no twitching mobile human face but as it were a mask with dignified, harmonious features; he does not cry out and does not even alter his voice; when a heavy thundercloud bursts upon him, he wraps himself up in his cloak and with slow and measured step walks away from beneath it.

1. Reprinted from *The Complete Works of Friedrich Nietzsche* Vol. II *Early Greek Philosophy and Other Essays* trans. by M. A. Mugge under general editorship of Dr. Oscar Levy [1909-1911]. New York: Russell & Russell 1964.

2. The German poet, Lessing, had been married for just a little over one year to Eva Konig. A son was born and died the same day, and the mother's life was despaired of. In a letter to his friend Eschenburg the poet wrote: ". . . and I lost him so unwillingly, this son! For he had so much understanding! so much understanding! Do not suppose that the few hours of fatherhood have made me an ape of a father! I know what I say. Was it not understanding, that they had to drag him into the world with a pair of forceps? that he so soon suspected the evil of this world? Was it not understanding, that he seized the first opportunity to get away from it? . . ." Eva Konig died a week later. — Tr.

3. In German *the tree — der Baum* — is masculine. —Tr.

4. In German *the plant — die Pflanze* — is feminine. —Tr.

5. *Cf.* the German *die Schlange* and *schlingen,* the English *serpent* from the Latin *serpere.* —Tr.

The Root Metaphor Theory of Metaphysics

Stephen C. Pepper

The root metaphor theory of metaphysics is a theory of the origin and development of metaphysical hypotheses. If correct, it entails certain consequences clarifying not only to the field of metaphysics but to other cognitive fields as well. It involves first (1), the proposition that dogmatism is illegitimate and unnecessary in cognitive procedure; second (2), that the method of hypothesis is legitimate, and so far as we can see, the only available undogmatic method; and, third (3), that one way, and perhaps the only way, in which metaphysical hypotheses can be derived is through the analysis of a selected group of facts (which I call the root metaphor) and the expansion of that analysis among other facts. The third proposition presupposes the first two, and the second the first; but the first proposition does not involve the other two, nor the second the third. One may eschew dogmatism and not champion a method of hypothesis, provided one can think of any other undogmatic cognitive method, but one may accept the method of hypothesis and not champion the root metaphor method, provided one can think of any other better hypothetical method by which metaphysical hypotheses may be derived. I will take the first two propositions up very briefly, for a thorough discussion of them would lead far beyond the bounds of a single paper, and I will spend my time mainly on the third. This paper, then, is an argument in the form: If the first two propositions are true, let me show you that the third proposition also is true — namely, that one way and perhaps the only way of legitimately developing a metaphysical hypothesis is by the root metaphor method.

The objection to dogmatism as a cognitive procedure is that it is a refusal to submit cognitive materials to cognitive scrutiny.

It is an assertion that such and such is true, or such and such is a fact, with an implicit or explicit threat of "hands off." Or it is similar assertions accompanied with a set of restrictions as to the sort of criticisms acceptable, such that automatically no hostile criticisms are acceptable. When brought out into the light in this way and plainly described, the position of dogmatism is seen to be intrinsically self-contradictory, for it is a way of attributing to materials cognitive values which these materials could receive only upon the application to them of cognitive criteria, and a refusal to permit these criteria to be applied.

The symptom of dogmatism is a refusal to permit certain materials to be doubted, and the subterfuge by means of which this refusal is legitimatized is to convert the particular form of refusal into a cognitive criterion. For example, the criterion suggested may be self-evidence — a term extraordinary enough in itself, for how could anything be evidence for itself? The evidence for a fact is other facts bearing upon it, causally or otherwise. Evidence in that sense is a genuine cognitive criterion (indeed, a whole set of criteria). But "self-evidence" is a way at once of acquiring the prestige of the criteria of evidence, and of dispensing with the need of applying them. Self-evidence is thus not a cognitive criterion at all, but precisely a refusal to permit a cognitive criterion to be applied.

One would think the exposure of such a subterfuge would be sufficient to banish it from use, but experience has shown otherwise. The more effective means is to show in the history of thought or in our own day contradictory facts (?) or principles which eminent men have asserted were self-evident or the equivalent. But there is not time to stop for this. On the basis of what I have said already, I must hope that you will agree with me that no dogmatic method is a legitimate cognitive method in metaphysics or anywhere else.

Now, if dogmatism is rejected, then any specific appeals by theories to self-evidence, certainty, indubitability, inconceivability, meaninglessness, and the like, are also rejected. The consequence of these rejections is to wipe the slate of cognitive methods amazingly clean. The traditional deductive method of discovering truths from the implication of self-evident axioms is obviously wiped away. But so, also, is the traditional inductive method of discovering reliable truths by generalizations from indubitable or stubborn facts. So, also, is the Descartian method of doubt, with its residue of indubitable facts, or the extension of his method to that limit known as the solipsism of the present moment. So, also, is the Kantian method of molding phenomena from *a priori* categories and forms of intuition. So also, the mystic method of dubbing unreal whatever is not a specific sort of feeling. And so, also, the positivistic method of dubbing meaningless whatever falls outside of an arbitrary definition of definition and meaning, or can not be stated in the form of atomic propositions. These are all methods of refusing to submit cognitive materials to cognitive scrutiny.

But it must not be thought that because all these methods are dogmatic and cognitively illegitimate, excellent cognitive results have not been attained by men employing these methods. On the contrary. And this fact brings out the point that even if dogmatic methods were legitimate, they are unnecessary. Perhaps the best way to exhibit this point is by reference to the two thoroughly intuitive views of traditional philosophy — mysticism, and solipsism of the present moment. Incidentally, the two views are mutually contradictory, and yet both are generally dogmatically supported on grounds of indubitable immediacy. But all I wish to point out here is that the substance of the two views is not changed an iota if the claims of indubitability are dropped. Offered as descriptions of the nature of things, a mystic or solipsistic *hypothesis* does not differ a bit from a mystic or solipsistic *dogma.* If either hypothesis is true, the corresponding intuition will be straight, of course. If the hypothesis is false, the intuition is illusory. There is no cognitive gain in insisting on the intuition. Dogmatism is, therefore, unnecessary. In fact, dogmatism has always in the history of thought been obstructive to cognitive advance, and the cognitive drive has come from a method of hypothesis. It is this method working beneath the dogmatisms of the great thinkers that has produced the advances in philosophy and science.

From the method of dogmatism I turn to the method of hypothesis, simply because I am not aware of any other undogmatic method. Though this method can be observed in its concrete operation through the whole history of thought, I am not sure that men have noticed what it involves when all dogmatic elements are cleared away.

In the first place, it involves the frank acceptance of the

situation that the origin of hypotheses is among uncriticized and therefore alterable facts. If anyone objects to the term "facts" denoting such entities, he may use any other term he pleases, but he must remember that facts denoting unalterable entities are at our present stage of knowledge purely ideal goals. Not that our perceptions, feelings, and immediacies may not be just what we perceive, feel, and intuit them to be, but that to assume certainty on these matters is dogmatic, and has frequently been shown to be unjustified in the history of thought. If we desire to be undogmatic, and unexposed in the rear of our cognitive endeavors, we must be prepared to change our minds about the reliability of any evidence whatever. Facts do not guarantee our hypotheses. Facts and hypotheses cooperate to guarantee the factuality and the truth of each other. Cognitive enterprises open in a field of uncriticized fact. How much of this field will remain unaltered as a result of critical scrutiny, one can not risk stating in advance. A constant recollection of this field of uncriticized fact, which quite correctly every hypothesis tries to abandon, is the greatest insurance against the fallacies of dogmatism. This field was called by Plato "opinion," by others it has been called common sense, or middle-sized fact, or pre-analytical fact.

In the second place, the method of hypothesis involves the acceptance of the criteria of scope and adequacy as the only general criteria for the factuality of fact or the truth of hypothesis. And the two criteria mutually support each other. By adequacy is meant the power of an hypothesis to give a description that apparently fits a fact or set of facts. The precise mode of fitting is at the discretion of the hypothesis and is part of the hypothesis. It may be correspondence, or coherence, or workability, or what you will. But whatever the mode of fitting is, the fit itself must be a good fit. It is not a good fit if some of the fact or some of the facts of the set are not included in the description; nor is it a good fit if two or more descriptions, both equally consistent with the hypothesis, can be given.[2] The fact itself, since it is not dogmatic or stubborn, can, of course, be molded or even disintegrated and distributed among other facts — whatever an hypothesis may demand. But a fact cannot be ignored. An adequate hypothesis may explain a fact away, but it may not leave a fact unexplained.

Adequacy alone, however, is not sufficient to determine the reliability of an hypothesis and its descriptions. For since it is dogmatic to assume that any limited description will be unaffected by outlying facts not included in that description, the determination of the reliability of that description can be reached only by obtaining descriptions of these outlying facts and observing whether or not the given description is affected. The greater the range of consistent descriptions the greater the assurance as to the adequacy of any given description. All of these mutually consistent and apparently adequate descriptions become evidence for one another, and render the fit of each particular description more ·firm. In short, scope increases adequacy. It follows, that the maximum of adequacy will be reached with the maximum of scope, namely, when the scope is all available facts whatever and the theory a world theory or a metaphysics.

In the third place, it must be apparent from the consequences already gleaned that a world hypothesis is informative of the nature of our world, or nothing is. There are notions prevalent that if judgments are derived from hypotheses they are merely hypothetical in a derogatory sense. Such notions, I believe, can only be held by people who retain a dogmatic faith in immediacies and stubborn facts. That faith, as I suggested, is cognitively quite unjustifiable, and once that faith is shaken, where can one turn for critical information about facts except to hypotheses and in the end to world hypotheses. Even utter skepticism is not an escape from this conclusion, for unless this doctrine is dogmatically held (and a dogmatic skepticism is no different from any other sort of dogmatism), the doctrine is subject to the same cognitive criticism as any other hypothesis and could not justify itself short of an examination of all available facts, in which case it becomes itself a world hypothesis.

So much, then, for the method of hypothesis. In the course of the foregoing discussion the prominent role of world hypotheses as our ultimate source for the discovery of the nature of facts comes to light. Now I want to ask: How do world hypotheses arise? And in answer to this question, I wish to suggest an hypothesis about world hypotheses, in order to glean therefrom a few more consequences relevant to the cognitive enterprise.

I will state the hypothesis without more ado. What I call the root metaphor theory is the theory that a world hypothesis to cover all facts is framed in the first instance on the basis of a rather small set of facts and then expanded in reference so as to cover all facts. The set of facts which inspired the hypothesis is the original root metaphor. It may be a ghost, or water, or air, or mutability, or qualitative composition, or mechanical push and pull, or the life history of youth, maturity, and age, or form and matter, or definition and similarity, or the mystic experience, or sensation, or the organic whole, or temporal process. Some of these facts in the course of expansion may prove adequate, others not. At first, they are accepted as they are found in uncriticized fact. How else could they be found? They are generally dogmatically assumed to be self-evident and indubitable. They are cognitively digested and analyzed. Their structure is usually found capable of rather wide extension through uncriticized facts not at first supposed to be of their nature. This structure is then elevated into an hypothesis for the explanation of other uncriticized facts, as a result of which these become critically interpreted in terms of the root metaphor. In the course of this interpretation, the root metaphor itself may undergo critical analysis and refinement which reciprocally increases its range and power of interpretation. When it assumes unlimited range, or world-wide scope, then it is a metaphysical hypothesis, and a catalogue of its principal descriptive concepts is a set of metaphysical categories.

That is the theory. Now, let me draw from this theory a number of consequences, which are not only interesting in themselves, but also the natural elaboration of the theory.

First, there develop alternative world theories based on different root metaphors. For while many root metaphors fail, a few expand into hypotheses of world-wide scope and great adequacy. These relatively fruitful root metaphors with their corresponding relatively adequate world hypotheses, I believe to be the following: similarity, which generates immanent realism; form and matter, which generates transcendent realism; push and pull, which generates mechanism; organic whole, which generates objective idealism; and temporal process, which generates contextualism (metaphysical pragmatism). None of these hypotheses is fully adequate. Whether in the hands of future ingenious philosophers one of them may turn out to be, nobody can very well say in advance. But it seems unlikely, since the inadequacies that arise within these philosophies are all of the form of self-contradictions. That is to say, the categories of each hypothesis lead to descriptions which both assert and deny something of certain facts. Such is the basis of the difficulty in the so-called problem of mind and matter in mechanism, and of the problem of the relation of the absolute to its fragments in objective idealism. There is always, of course, the chance that with refinement of the categories, the contradictory descriptions may disappear. But in such cases as the above where the difficulties are traceable directly back to the categories, and where the theories have been worked over by many men for many years, the chance seems slight of ironing out the source of the difficulties. The point is that we now have, and are likely to continue to have, no fully adequate world theory, but a number of alternative rather highly adequate world theories, each of which is able to describe or interpret any presented fact, criticized or uncriticized, but each of which contains some internal ulcer of self-contradiction.

Second, the foregoing situation does not justify anyone in rejecting any or all of these theories in default of a better. The rejection of all but one of these theories and the retention of that, is too obviously dogmatic to need exhibition. Yet this method of exclusion is one of the commonest methods for justifying a preferred theory. The inadequacies of theories A, B, and C are carefully shown. That leaves only theory D, which is then sympathetically exposed. The unwary reader may never suspect that the inadequacies of D are as great as those of A, B, and C. The inadequacies of other world theories are no evidence for a given world theory.

Moreover, a sweeping rejection of all world theories as cognitively worthless because they are all demonstrably somewhat inadequate, is also dogmatic. It must not be forgotten that the denial of a theory, in so far as the denial has any cognitive significance, is also a theory. And this theory that no world theories have any cognitive value, has, in view of the several relatively adequate world theories we know, very little adequacy — only as much, to be precise, as any one of these theories has inadequacy. It is as weak as the strongest world theory is strong. The only facts this theory can describe adequately are the facts the most adequate theory cannot describe adequately. As a theory, then, in competition with relatively adequate theories, this theory is not tenable — a result which merely indicates in an abstract way the concrete fact that utter skepticism in the face of the large amount of corroborative knowledge we possess is a ridiculous theory. And a skepticism which refuses to examine the evidences of knowledge is sheer dogmatism.

The second point, then, is that the admitted inadequacies of the several relatively adequate world hypotheses is not a good reason for the rejection of all or any of them; but on the contrary, since they are all in the same condition, a reason for the retention of them all. Presumably each gives some sort of information about the world the others garble.

Third, each of the alternative relatively adequate theories gives a different and irreconcilable description from the others of the "same" fact. Let the fact be any uncriticized fact — say, voluntary action, this fact is critically described in one way by a mechanist, in quite another way by an idealist. There can be no question about the difference between the two descriptions. And the more the reasons for the discrepancies are looked into the more obvious appears the irreconcilability of the descriptions, for the differences have their source in the categories of the two world theories, and these two sets of categories show no sign of ever converging into a single set of categories. Moreover, neither of these descriptions can be discarded in favor of the other, since, so far as we can see, the two world theories are about equally adequate.

Can we avoid the difficulty by saying that the two descriptions cover different facts, or cover different aspects or relations of a fact? Two people describe different sides of the same coin, or, having different esthetic interests, describe different features of the same painting. Each description is true but partial, and all are reconcilable because, strictly speaking, every description was of a different fact. At first, and to a degree, this explanation would seem to apply to our metaphysical situation. It is admitted that the uncriticized fact, from which the two metaphysical descriptions start, is not certain or stubborn, and is to a degree molded and metamorphosed by the two categorial interpretations. By the time the analyses are finished, the facts intended as well as the descriptions may be totally different.

But this explanation is weakened, when we realize that a relatively adequate world theory describes not only uncriticized facts but also the criticized facts of other world theories, for its adequacy depends on its capacity to interpret any facts whatever. The idealist will, then, have his explanation of the error in the mechanist's description of voluntary action, and vice versa. If either description has so far transformed the uncriticized fact that the latter is unrecognizable in the former, the critic is sure to bring this out and gloat over the discovery. Rarely, he succeeds in doing this, as when a mechanist is caught identifying the quality of a sound with air waves, but the greatness of the jubilee when this does occur is evidence that it does not often occur. Clearly, it could not occur often without jeopardizing the adequacy of the theory that did it, for it amounts to a failure to describe a fact. But the point I am here making is that even if the two descriptions of the uncriticized fact so far diverged from each other as to become descriptions of different facts, the divergence would be filled in as soon as each of the theories described each other's descriptions, for an adequate description of a description involves consideration of what that description was about.

And whatever plausibility may yet remain for the idea that alternative metaphysical descriptions supposedly of the same fact are actually about different facts, evaporates when one considers the alternative theories as total descriptions. The total mass of facts presented for description to each world theory is the same total mass on any interpretation of "same." Any fact, part, aspect, or relation which may have escaped description in considering a theory problem by problem, does not escape in the total systematic consideration of a theory. Take the spread of description wide enough, and two relatively adequate world theories are bound to cover any given field of fact, and their descriptions of this field will be different and irreconcilable.

Fourth, alternative equally adequate world theories are autonomous. One world theory can not legitimately judge a description of another world theory as wrong simply because the description of the latter is not such as the former would have made. For this kind of judgment assumes that one set of categories is right and other sets wrong, which is, without a sympathetic consideration of the other theory, a dogmatic assumption. The justification for such general legislative powers is often claimed on the basis that a given world theory can explain or include in itself the other theories. But so can and must any relatively adequate world theory. Other theories are among the most important facts that any world theory must interpret. Failure in interpreting would constitute a great inadequacy in an interpreting theory, but success in interpreting has no effect upon an interpreted theory. The adequacy of a theory can not, therefore, be judged by any alien theory.

Neither can it be judged by any other external agency — unless facts be regarded as external to a theory, and even these are not stubborn. Is there not truth and logic? Every world theory has its own theory of truth and its own logic. What about a logical calculus, such as a calculus of propositions? As a fact, of course, every world theory must accept such a calculus and interpret it; but as an ultimate canon of right reasoning, such a calculus is far from acceptable to many theories. Even such general logical principles as identity and contradiction acquire quite different concrete interpretations from theory to theory, and if anything strictly unaltered remains over for these principles in all theories, this is simply due to the fact that each set of categories generates them. The validity of these principles depends on the fruitfulness of the hypotheses which employ them, not the reverse. To assert their self-evidence or their validity independent of their function in hypotheses, would be dogmatic.

Each world theory develops its own cognitive canons out of its own categories, and by these canons judges its own adequacy. That is to say, the contradictions which develop in a theory, are contradictions in the theory's own terms. Idealistic logic itself, for instance, offers no means of harmonizing the finite and the absolute. A world theory is autonomous in its interpretations of facts and autonomous in its criticism of its interpretations. This does not mean that an idealist is always the best critic of idealism, but that, whoever the critic may be, the only legitimate criticism of idealism is in idealistic terms.

Fifth, eclecticism is confusing. By the root metaphor conception we are able to give a precise definition of eclecticism. It is an attempt to interpret facts by means of incompatible sets of categories, categories generated from different root metaphors. Eclecticism is, therefore, mixed metaphor. A specious richness of connotation is obtained thereby at the sacrifice of clarity. I hesitate to say that it is always fallacious. In cases where the inadequacy of a world theory lies in its inability to describe a certain type or group of facts, it may well be claimed that a more complete total theory is obtained by borrowing for this group of facts the categories of another root metaphor. But it must be remembered that the adequacy of the descriptions of this borrowed set can only be determined by the scope (that is, range of descriptive power) of that set. In other words, the borrowed set of categories can be relied upon to furnish a relatively adequate description of the limited group of facts only because it has a capacity of describing a much larger group of facts than the group it is called on to describe; it may even be able to describe all facts. Why not, then, go over to the descriptions of the borrowed set throughout, and abandon the descriptions of the first set, which lack scope? The only plausible reason why this should not be done is that the second set may lack scope in a region of fact where the first set appears to be adequate. But even then, the intermediate regions of fact, which both theories claim to describe with adequacy, will be permeated with ambiguity and confusion. Is it not better to keep the two theories well apart, study the descriptions which each give separately, and note the regions which each is able to describe but the other not?

Actually, however, such considerations as these, as to what should be done in cases where theories lack scope, are of little more than academic interest, for we possess several theories of world-wide scope, and, the dogma of the stubborn fact being set aside, these world theories automatically supplant hypotheses of limited scope. This must not, incidentally, be interpreted to mean that hypotheses applying to a limited number of facts are necessarily hypotheses of limited scope. Every world hypothesis generates a nest of sub-hypotheses for the purpose of describing limited ranges of fact. But since these sub-hypotheses are all derivable from the main hypothesis, they possess indirectly the scope of that main hypothesis. They are not hypotheses of limited scope.

Sixth and last, as the reverse of eclectic confusion, the root metaphor conception offers a means of obtaining clarity in metaphysics. Once the few fruitful root metaphors have been intuited and the characteristic behavior of their sets of categories in description noted, then it is possible to untangle complex philosophic writings, to judge the feasible mode of solution or the very solubility of given problems, and to determine the bearing and validity of philosophic criticisms.

I offer this theory in the first place as a description of fact, as a statement of what philosophers consciously or unconsciously always have done in their attempt to understand the world in which they live. The method expounded by this theory underlies, I maintain, all dogmatisms, and is presupposed by all eclecticisms. And in the second place, whether the theory be correct in fact or not, I offer it as a useful instrument for the clarification of a confused field.

1. Reprinted from *Journal of Philosophy* 32 (1935) 365-374.

2. I am assuming here that the cause of the alternative mutually inconsistent descriptions is some indeterminateness in the governing concepts of the hypothesis, not an insufficiency of facts. In the latter case, it is not the hypothesis that is inadequate, but the facts; and the proper cognitive thing to do in the absence of sufficient facts is to make as many alternative descriptions or sub-hypotheses as one can, consistent with the main hypothesis and such facts as one has. Then one knows as much as one can know, under the circumstances, about the facts concerned.

Metaphor

John Middleton Murry

Discussions of metaphor — there are not many of them —
often strike us at first as superficial. Not until we have ourselves
made the attempt to get further do we begin to realize that the
investigation of metaphor is curiously like the investigation of
any of the primary data of consciousness: it cannot be pursued
very far without our being led to the borderline of sanity.
Metaphor is as ultimate as speech itself, and speech as ultimate
as thought. If we try to penetrate them beyond a certain point,
we find ourselves questioning the very faculty and instrument
with which we are trying to penetrate them. The earth trembles
and yawns beneath the explorer's feet. *Medio tutissimus ibis;*
but the middle way is hard to find.

Suppose we take a familiar metaphor, as that the fiery spirit
of Emily Bronte burned up her body. It cannot fairly be called
cliche; it is rather a familiar and necessary idiom. Necessary,
because we find that there is no way of saying what we want to
say about Emily Bronte save by this metaphor or one of its
variations. This obvious necessity of the metaphor, this absence
of genuine alternatives, seems to make it clear that so soon as
one person perceived in another and sought to describe such a
quality as Emily Bronte's, a kindred metaphor was forced upon
him. We may even say that the quality could not have been
perceived without the metaphor. The imagination that the soul
inhabits the body as fire inhabits the material which it burns
must surely go back to the moment when the existence of the
soul was first surmised; for only by such an image could the
nature of the soul's existence be at all apprehended. And we
may leave it undecided, or as impossible of decision, whether
the creation of the metaphor was the result of a search for a

27

description of the previously felt existence of the soul, or the existence of the soul was suggested by the manner of the flame's existence.

For, whichever it may have been, and perhaps the processes were equally prevalent, metaphor appears as the instinctive and necessary act of the mind exploring reality and ordering experience. It is the means by which the less familiar is assimilated to the more familiar, the unknown to the known: it 'gives to airy nothing a local habitation and a name,' so that it ceases to be airy nothing. To attempt a fundamental examination of metaphor would be nothing less than an investigation of the genesis of thought itself — a dangerous enterprise. Therefore we instinctively seek to circumscribe our own inquiries by leaving out of account as far as may be the countless host of dead or dormant metaphors of which the most part of language is composed, and concentrating on the living ones. We take for granted the past exploration of reality of which dead and dormant metaphors are the record, and try to focus our minds on the present, hazardous, incomplete, and thrilling exploration of reality which is represented by metaphors which still retain their vitality.

Such are the metaphors of what we call creative literature. These remain alive because they are the records of an exploration of reality by men who stood head and shoulders above their fellows, who discerned resemblances between the unknown and the known which the generality could not accept nor common speech assimilate. Their metaphors are felt still to be the vehicle of some immediate revelation to those who attend to them. As Aristotle said, 'But the greatest thing of all by far is to be a master of metaphor. It is the one thing that cannot be learned from others; and it is also a sign of original genius, since a good metaphor implies the intuitive perception of the similarity in dissimilars.' The statement, made so long ago, seems final still.

But before we hazard a small attempt to advance from it towards Coleridge's discussion of imagery, we need to inquire, for the sake of clarity, whether there is any but a formal difference between metaphor and simile and image. 'Far out, as though idly, listlessly, gulls were flying. Now they settled on the waves, now they beat up into the rainy air, *and shone against the pale sky like the lights within a pearl.*' The last words would be called indifferently an image or a simile. Change them to 'shining lights in the pale pearl of sky,' it becomes — not by any means to its advantage, for a reason we may discover — a metaphor. But the act of creative perception remains the same. And it seems impossible to regard metaphors and similes as different in any essential property: metaphor is compressed simile. The word 'image' however, which has come to usurp a prominent place in these discussions, is more recalcitrant. It not only narrows the content of the word 'simile,' but tends to force unduly into the foreground the part played by the visual image. In the beautiful simile quoted above the visual image is preponderant; in Baudelaire's agonizing one:

> *Ces affreuses nuits*
> *Qui compriment le coeur comme un papier qu'on froisse,*

the visual image has no part at all. Again, it is obvious foolishness to persuade oneself that any visual image underlies the magnificent metaphors —

> Thou still unravish'd bride of quietness:
> Thou foster-child of Silence and slow Time.

Yet though the suggestion of the word 'image' is dangerous, the word is necessary. For metaphor and simile belong to formal classification. The word 'image,' precisely because it is used to cover both metaphor and simile, can be used to point towards their fundamental identity; and if we resolutely exclude from our minds the suggestion that the image is solely or even predominantly visual, and allow the word to share in the heightened and comprehensive significance with which its derivative 'imagination' has perforce been endowed — if we conceive the 'image' not as primary and independent, but as the most singular and potent instrument of the faculty of imagination — it is a more valuable word than those which it subsumes: metaphor and simile. To them clings something worse than false suggestion: a logical taint, an aura of irrelevancy.

The image may be visual, may be auditory, may refer back to any primary physical experience — as those hoary metaphors which describe the process of thought itself as a grasping or apprehension — or it may be wholly psychological, the reference of one emotional or intellectual experience to another, as

> Then felt I like some watcher of the skies
> When a new planet swims into his ken . . .

The essential is simply that there should be that intuitive
perception of similarity between dissimilars of which Aristotle
speaks. What we primarily demand is that the similarity should
be a true similarity and that it should have lain hitherto
unperceived, or but rarely perceived by us, so that it comes to
us with an effect of revelation: something hitherto unknown is
suddenly made known. To that extent the image is truly
creative: it marks an advance, for the writer who perceives and
the reader who receives it, in the conquest of some reality.

We also in our inquiry may take a step forward. That we
demand more of imagery than this may be seen in our
instinctive refusal of the image of a modern prose-writer, who
speakes of the 'churches, like shapes of grey paper, breasting the
stream of the Strand.' There are two images, and they war with
each other. If the churches really breasted the stream of the
Strand, they were not at that moment like shapes of grey paper.

Possibly both perceptions are valid in isolation; in association
they nullify one another. Yet how often does Shakespeare seem
to commit the same offence.

> It is great
> To do that thing that ends all other deeds:
> Which shackles accident, and bolts up change;
> Which sleeps, and never palates more the dug,
> The beggar's nurse and Caesar's.

Yet the offence is only apparent. The images do not in fact
disturb each other, whereas the modern writer's images do. This
is partly because in the modern writer's imagery the stress lies
wholly upon the visual: if we do not see what we are required
to see, the sentence fails of its effect; and partly because of the
characteristic swiftness of Shakespeare's language. We have not,
and we are not intended to have, time to unfold his metaphors;
and, moreover, the boldest and most abrupt transition among
them is in its effect the smoothest. For the rhythm leaves no
doubt that it is not 'the dug' but Death that is 'the beggar's

nurse and Caesar's.' Death, which in the previous line was the child sleeping against the heart, becomes the bosom that receives mankind. We may say it is the mere verbal suggestion that links the metaphors. Yet, though it is true that verbal 'self-suggestion' is potent in high poetry ('Forlorn! the very word is like a knell . . .'), it seems truer in this case to say that the one metaphor grows immediately out of the other. It is as though the vague 'thing,' from which the images take their rise, swiftly groped after shapes before our mind's eye, and finally achieved a full realization — 'the beggar's nurse and Caesar's.'

This is the work of the greatest of all masters of metaphor, and it would be preposterous to try others' achievement by its standard. The self-creative progress of Shakespeare's imagery is a thing apart. But by comparing small things with great we may see that the internal harmony which the modern writer fails to secure is a necessary quality of true imagery. Shakespeare's methods of securing it are indeed startling; he takes what seem to be impossible risks, and wins with ease. His success, when we examine it, is not really so surprising, for the extent to which images are discordant depends upon the extent we unfold them, and that is wholly within the great poet's control, for it in turn depends primarily upon the rhythm and tempo of his writing. And this, more than any other, is the reason why the successful use of metaphor is very much bolder in poetry than in prose. The poet's means of control — that is to say, the possibilities of tempo and rhythm in poetry — are much richer and more flexible than in prose. He has our sensibilities, our powers of realization and comparison, far more completely under his thumb than the prose-writer. So that we may hazard a generalization and say that the creative simile is by nature more appropriate to prose than the creative metaphor. Prose gives us time to bear upon the comparison, which if it be exact and revealing, will stand the strain of our attention, and is better frankly exposed to the inquiry it must receive. And, again, the function of imagery in poetry differs perceptibly from the function of imagery in prose. In poetry metaphor is chiefly a means to excite in us a vague and heightened awareness of qualities we can best call spiritual. Exactness and precision are seldom sought, and, if they are, are seldom valuable; and often where an apparent exactness exists, as in the Homeric simile, it is an incidental exactness and does not reinforce the point of specific analogy. Set two equally famous heroic portraits by great poets against each other.

> His legs bestrid the ocean; his rear'd arm
> Crested the world: his voice was propertied
> As all the tuned spheres, and that to friends;
> But when he meant to quail, and shake the orb,
> He was as rattling thunder. For his bounty,
> There was no winter in't; an autumn 'twas
> That grew the more by reaping: his delights
> Were dolphin-like; they show'd his back above
> The element they liv'd in: in his livery
> Walk'd crowns and crownets; realms and islands were
> As plates dropp'd from his pocket . . .

>   He above the rest
> In shape and gesture proudly eminent
> Stood like a Tower, his form had not yet lost
> All her original brightness, nor appear'd
> Less than archangel ruin'd, and th' excess
> Of glory obscur'd, as when the sun new risen
> Looks through the horizontal misty air
> Shorn of his beams; or from behind the moon
> In dim eclipse disastrous twilight sheds
> On half the nations; and with fear of change
> Perplexes monarchs.

The Miltonic tempo, as ever, is far slower than Shakespeare's; therefore we bear more heavily upon his comparisons, and in sufficient measure they stand the strain; but the whole effect is not precise, but rather vague, vast, and foreboding. So also, in its totally different kind, the picture of Antony that is impressed upon our minds is of some thing (rather than some one) immense, generous, genial, a careless and overflowing force of nature — a dynamic phenomenon as peculiar to Shakespeare's view of the universe as the static figure of Satan to Milton's. Exactness of this kind there is in both; but it comes not from the exactness of the particular comparisons, it is a total effect of many comparisons, as it were a painting of one great and indefinable quality by many strokes of minor yet allied analogies. To evoke such elemental spirits is seldom the purpose of prose, nor of the imagery proper to it. It also seizes, in so far as it is creative, indefinable qualities, but they are more specific and more local.

Soon after daybreak we were streaming down the arrowy Rhone, at the rate of twenty miles an hour, in a very dirty vessel full of merchandise, and with only three or four other passengers for our companions: among whom the most remarkable was a silly old, meek-faced, garlic-eating, immeasurably polite Chevalier, with a dirty scrap of red ribbon at his buttonhole, *as if he had tied it there to remind him of something.*

It is perfect, it gives us the man — an individual and comic inhabitant of earth. Perhaps as an example it suggests that the prose use of simile must be more prosaic than we mean to imply. We have quoted solely to point an essential difference between the imagery of prose and poetry. The imagery of poetry is in the main complex and suggestive; the imagery of prose single and explicit.

But the three examples serve also to illustrate what is the highest function of imagery — namely, to define indefinable spiritual qualities. All metaphor and simile can be described as the analogy by which the human mind explores the universe of quality and charts the non-measurable world. Of these indefinite qualities some are capable of direct sensuous apprehension, while others can be grasped only by a faculty which, though obviously akin to sensuous apprehension, yet differs from it. Sensuous perception is of the qualities of the visible, audible, tangible world; of the spiritual qualities of the more recondite world of human personality and its creations there is intuition. Both faculties are necessary to the great poet, but there have been many who, though richly gifted with sensuous perception, have been deficient or altogether lacking in spiritual intuition. To the great poet his constant accumulation of vivid sense-perceptions supplies the most potent means by which he articulates his spiritual intuitions, for recognitions of spiritual quality can be most forcefully and swiftly conveyed through analogous recognitions of sensuous quality. One has only to imagine how much, and how much in vain, another writer might toil to render the quality of Antony that is given once for all in the words, grammatically confused though they are: —

>   ... his delights
> Were dolphin-like; they show'd his back above
> The element they lived in ...

or to consider the pregnant subtlety of these two kindred images:

>   This common body,
> Like to a vagabond flag upon the stream,
> Goes to and back, lackeying the varying tide,
> To rot itself with motion. . . .

> Her tongue will not obey her heart, nor can
> Her heart inform her tongue, — the swan's down-feather,
> That stands upon the swell at full of tide
> And neither way inclines . . .

to realize the enormous resources for describing the subtlest nuances of emotion and character which a vivid percipience of the sensuous world can give.

But the greatest mastery of imagery does not lie in the use, however beautiful and revealing, of isolated images, but in the harmonious total impression produced by a succession of subtly related images. In such cases the images appear to grow out of one another and to be fulfilling an independent life of their own. Yet this apparent autonomy is as strictly subordinated to a final impression as the steps of a logical argument are to their conclusion. Such triumphs of imagery are to be conceived as a swift and continuous act of exploration of the world of imagination — though an obvious metaphor is in that phrase. A magnificent example of this peculiar movement of mind on a scale so large that it can be carefully examined is Keats's *Ode to a Nightingale.* The strange combination of imaginative autonomy and profound total harmony in that poem is characteristic of the movement of creative imagery in its highest forms. We can perhaps get a clear glimpse of the nature of this contradictory process of creative imagery — the maximum of independence combined with the most complete and pervasive subordination — in one of the rare moments when we can honestly claim to be able to look over Shakespeare's shoulder. The famous picture of Cleopatra on Cydnus comes substantially from North's Plutarch, of which the following sentence is the original of Shakespeare's first seven lines:

> She disdained to set forward otherwise, but to take her barge in the river of Cydnus, the poope whereof was of gold, the sails of purple, and the owers of silver, which kept stroke in rowing after the sound of flutes, howboys, cytherns, violls, and such other instruments as they played upon the barge . . .

It is often said that Shakespeare followed North as closely as he could, with the minimum of original effort. It is not true. North's sentence would fall quite easily into good blank verse, but it would be nothing like —

> *The barge she sat in, like a burnish'd throne,*
> *Burn'd on the water:* the poop was beaten gold;
> Purple the sails, *and so perfumed that*
> *The winds were love-sick with them;* the oars were silver,
> Which to the tune of flutes, kept stroke, *and made*
> *The water which they beat to follow faster,*
> *As amorous of their strokes . . .*

The phrases in italics are Shakespeare's additions: afterwards he keeps more closely to North until he comes to the climax. North has it:

> Others also rann out of the city to see her coming in. So that in the end, there rann such multitudes of people one after another, that *Antonius* was left post alone in the market-place, in his Imperiall seate to give audience.

Which is transformed into:

> The city cast
> Her people out upon her, and Antony,
> Enthron'd in the market-place, did sit alone,
> *Whistling to the air: which, but for vacancy,*
> *Had gone to gaze on Cleopatra too*
> *And made a gap in nature.*

The additions are worth attention. North's somewhat amorphous prose is given a beginning and an end. The additions are all, in spite of formal differences, essentially similes and metaphors; and, after the first, which gathers the vision into one whole which it puts imperishably before the mind's eye, the second and third develop the theme which is clinched in climax by the fourth. In them the successive elements — the winds, the water, the air — are represented all as succumbing to the enchantment of love which breathes from the great Queen and her burning barge; and by this varied return on a single motive North's inconsequential panorama is given an organic unity. It is quite impossible to conceive Shakespeare as dovetailing old and new together. Before his mind's eye as he read North had risen a picture half visible, half spiritual, in short, truly imaginative — the manifestation of Egypt, before whom the elements made obeisance. All of North that was congruous with his enchanted vision he incorporated with a flowing pen into his new creation. And the added imagery, about which he probably took no second thought, grew natually into harmony with itself and with the whole.

To this strange but strangely natural process Coleridge was referring in his often-quoted and sometimes violently interpreted words:

Images, however beautiful, though faithfully copied from nature, and as accurately represented in words, do not of themselves characterize the poet. They become proofs of original genius only in so far as they are modified by a predominant passion, or by associated thoughts and images awakened by that passion; or when they have the effect of reducing multitude to unity, or succession to an instant; or lastly when a human and intellectual life is transferred to them from the poet's own spirit.

Instances, and better instances than Coleridge himself gives, of all the qualities which he demands of truly creative imagery are to be found in the picture of Cleopatra. 'Multitude is reduced to unity' by the first of the added images; and in the other three a human and intellectual life is transferred to the images (Coleridge should perhaps have said, to the objects of the images) from the poet's own spirit. This last desideratum had been put forward long before by Aristotle in his discussion of 'vividness' in the *Rhetoric*. Vividness, he there says, depends upon metaphor and on 'setting things before the eyes'; but 'setting things before the eyes' turns out itself to be a metaphor, and not, as one might imagine, a demand for the visual image.

'This is my definition,' says Aristotle:

> Those words set a thing before the eyes which describe it in an active state . . . Or we may use the device often employed by Homer of giving life to lifeless things by means of metaphor. In all such cases he wins applause by describing an active state, as in the line

> Back to the plain rolled the shameless stone.

Whether the process is described thus dryly as by Aristotle, or more transcendentally by Coleridge, as the working of the poetic spirit 'which shoots its being through earth, sea, and air,' the fact is indubitable. It seems to be an imperious need of the creative spirit of the poet to impart life to the apparently lifeless. This may appear a 'device' in the cold light of analysis; but nothing is more certain than that when it is used as a device it is intolerable. No conscious contrivance produced 'Thou still unravish'd bride of quietness,' or 'Joy, whose hand is ever at his lips, Bidding adieu.' Such things as these — and how many of the most magnificently natural achievements of poetry belong to this kind — are, beyond all doubt, the effect of some 'silent working of the spirit.' By the intensity of the poet's contemplation the lifeless thing lives indeed.

Probably the world of true imagination of which these miracles are the common substance is for ever inviolable by intellectual analysis. Even to apprehend its subject-matter the intellect must suffer a sea-change, so that it is no longer itself and cannot perform its proper function. Restore its power to the intellect again, and that which it seeks to understand has ceased to exist as what it really is. This world of imagination is a universe wherein quality leaps to cohere with quality across the abysms of classification that divide and categorize the universe of intellectual apprehension. Its true citizens are few and far between; they are the masters of metaphor, and the authentic messages they bring from that near yet distant country perplex our brains and comfort our souls with the half-assurance that the things that are may be otherwise than as we know them.

Towards this exalted region, as to the sole reality, Coleridge was ever groping; and what he meant by the 'predominant passion' which modifies the images of original genius is the power by which genius comprehends its chosen region of this world of qualitative interpenetration. The passion is a passionate contemplation of the unity which pervades the chosen region: a creative passion to correspond with an organic unity. Whether the unity proceeds from the passion, or the passion from the unity, it would be profitless to inquire. They are knit together, as knower and known, in one act of creative comprehension. But if we are shy of the notion of Coleridge which seems to give the poetic spirit an actually plastic power over the material world, we have only to reflect that the predominant passion of the poet's mind is but the counterpart of a predominant quality of the region of the universe which he contemplates. His passion roused by the quality is reflected back upon the quality, and gives it redoubled power; so that it begins to dominate all other qualities and properties, to suffuse them with itself till it becomes as it were the living and governing soul of that which the poet contemplates. By means of his passion the actual realizes its own idea.

However much we struggle, we cannot avoid transcendentalism, for we are seeking to approximate to a universe of quality with analogy for its most essential language through a universe of quantity with a language of identities. Sooner or later, a transcendentalism (which is only the name for a prodigious metaphor) is inevitable. But the process may be brought a little closer to the light of common day if we take once more that region of the qualitative universe which Shakespeare embodied in Cleopatra. She was, we may say, the incarnation of love: the mighty, elemental power which, in Shakespeare's experience, was love, was made corporeal in her. She is possessed by it; from her it radiates and compels obeisance from the elements. But she is not merely a contemplated but a self-uttering thing; and this power that informs her body informs her soul also. All her thoughts are shaped by it. Without her love she will die, she must die; but when she imagines death, she imagines it as a consummation of love, as the thing

> Which sleeps, and never palates more the dug,
> The beggar's nurse and Caesar's . . .

She dies, and her dying she imagines as a reliving of her triumph on Cydnus. 'I am again for Cydnus, to meet Mark Antony.' And it is a more wonderful triumph. 'Yare, yare, good Iras.' The flower-soft hands that yarely framed the office frame one last office more; and at the aspic's touch the Queen is wholly dedicate to the love she is and serves. The winds, the water, the air obeyed on Cydnus; now the most fickle element of all obeys — her own secret self, from which well up the images of love in death, and death in love:

> The stroke of death is as a lover's pinch
> That hurts and is desired . . .
>   Peace, peace!
> Dost thou not see my baby at my breast
> That sucks the nurse asleep?

In the intensity of Shakespeare's imagination the great property takes utter and complete possession of that it dwells in. By the alchemy of Cleopatra's images death is transmuted into a sleep of love. But her thoughts are Shakespeare's thoughts, her predominant passion his. Therefore it is not strange that Caesar, who in the waking world knows nothing of her dying words, should echo them, and prolong her triumph beyond her death.

>   She looks like sleep,
>   As she would catch another Antony
>   In her strong toil of grace.

But Caesar did not know what Shakespeare knew, that it was the self-same Antony whom she had taken.

1. Permission to include this essay has been granted by The Society of Authors as the literary representative of the Estate of John Middleton Murry. This essay was written in 1927.

Imagery: From Sensation to Symbol

Norman Friedman

Imagery has come to mean all things to all men. How else could books with such various aims, methods, and results have been entitled as similarly as *Shakespeare's Imagery,*[2] *Shakespeare's World of Images,*[3] *The Development of Shakespeare's Imagery,*[4] and *Shakespeare's Imagination?*[5] Such a variety of meanings implies on the one hand perhaps a healthy humanistic pluralism, or on the other perhaps a real semantic muddle. What I want to suggest is not that we must agree upon only one meaning of this protean word and then fasten it permanently on the dry and sandy beach of narrow exactitude, but rather that we must catalogue its different shapes if we are to know with whom we have to deal when encountering it in its own watery element. A charting of the coast is long overdue.

The method of this essay is at once historical and programmatic, dealing with the uses to which the word has been put as well as those to which it ought now to be put. These tend to fall into three more or less clearly distinguishable, if interdependent, categories, which can be arranged in progressive order: (1) mental or physiological, (2) rhetorical, and (3) symbolic imagery. Thus it can be seen, even from this crude breakdown, that the study of poetic imagery represents a point formed by the intersection of many, often divergent, lines of inquiry. The fixing of that point is, in addition, often complicated by the fact that these lines are not seen by all to cross at the same juncture — if at all. The first category, for example, is largely concerned with the psychology of perception; the second with the theory of metaphor and its tributaries — philology, etymology, aesthetics, and semantics; while the last embraces cultural anthropology and comparative

41

mythology as its own.

About the close of the last and the beginning of the present century, articles began appearing with increasing frequency in the psychological journals bearing such titles as "Mental Imagery — Experimentally and Subjectively Considered,"[6] "Methods of Determining Ideational Types,"[7] "The Imaginal Reaction to Poetry,"[8] "Imagery and Mentality,"[9] or "The Function of Images in the Appreciation of Poetry."[10] The basic concern here was the relation of the word on the page to the sensation produced by it in the mind's "eye." There developed a fatal fascination for testing the mind's image-predispositions and capacities on all levels, mainly as a result of the stimulus provided by the experiments of Sir Francis Galton (1822-1911), who discovered that people differed in their image-making habits ('how much of your breakfast-table can you recall to mind and describe now?' the questionnaires ran).[11] Thus, while one person may reveal a predominating tendency to visualize his reading, memories, and ruminations (as indeed many of us do), another may favor the mind's "ear," another the mind's "nose," or yet another may have no imagery at all.

These investigations caught the interest of a number of poetically-minded psychologists who tried to determine the function of mental imagery in the comprehension and enjoyment of literature. The question is in reality two-fold: (1) can we assume that the same poem arouses the same degree and kind of imagery in the minds of a variety of readers? and (2) if not, must we conclude that those having the stronger imaginal capacities are (at least potentially) better readers of poetry? or that those of the visualizing type are better than those of the auditory type? and so on.

The pedagogic implications of such questions are far-reaching, for if one student is born with a vivid sense of mental imagery and another without, and if adequate testing devices were to be made available, then the problem of who should study literature, who philosophy, and who engineering, could be solved simply by referring to the proper set of statistics.

Such psychometric precision is fortunately not forthcoming. George Herbert Betts concluded, after conducting an exhaustive series of statistical tests, that not only does mental imagery play a much smaller role in the comprehension and enjoyment of poetry than had hitherto been assumed (and often is still assumed), but also that an excessive concern over such imagery can actually impede pleasure and understanding. Poetry, as he says, also operates via "meaning, feeling, and sentiment."[12]

Next, the question arises: if we cannot classify readers in any significant manner regarding their literary capacities, can we nevertheless use the image-tabulation method as a way of developing a sounder, more objective critical approach; as a way, that is, of fixing more accurately the intrinsic nature of the work of any given poet? In attempting an answer, we find ourselves perched back on the horns of the old dilemma —*who* shall do the counting? An image which appears obviously tactile to me, for example, may seem clearly motor to you. June E. Downey suggested, however, that perhaps more readers reporting upon larger portions of text might improve the reliability of such statistics.[13]

By the 1920's, literary critics such as Bliss Perry[14] and John Kester Bonnell[15] were discriminating among the various types of mental images and were arguing for a more tolerant approach toward the work of poets whose imagery predispositions happen to be different from our own. Much of Browning's imagery, for example, is tactile, and those who are eye-minded are unjust in laying the charge of obscurity at his door.

The only strictly literary application of the psychology of perception to the detailed examination of poetry which I have seen is Richard Harter Fogle's study of Keats and Shelley.[16] His primary purpose is to defend Shelley against the strictures of certain modern critics who would persuade us that he is "abstract" and "evanescent," as opposed to Keats, who is "rich" and "concrete." He bases his argument upon a statistical chart listing the comparative percentile ratings (ratio of images to lines) of the two poets, having been influenced in the main by Miss Downey. He discovers that the differences between Keats and Shelley are statistically less spectacular than we have been led to believe. With regard to visual, auditory, olfactory, gustatory, and kinesthetic imagery, there are no important differences. In tactual and organic imagery, however, Keats is higher, while Shelley leads in motor imagery. The conclusion, therefore, is that if Shelley's imagery is different in kind, it is no less intense in degree.

Beginning with the work of the redoubtable Max Muller, whose lectures on "The Science of Languages" were delivered at the Royal Institution in 1861-64, the nature of metaphor —

hitherto almost categorized out of existence by the traditional rhetoricians — became once again an open question. Metaphors (and other related "figures of speech") present a peculiarly acute problem in the study of the poetic image since they involve "images" almost explicitly arranged to serve a symbolic function. That is, the images in metaphors are, by definition, no longer literal. This issue was either not considered or was left obscured by the investigators discussed above (with the possible exception of Miss Downey), and we may assume that "mental" and "metaphorical" images were covertly lumped together under a single heading.

The distinction had to be made, however, and, as we shall see below, must continue to be made. The central question here is: how do metaphors come into being? and further, how do they die — how can we account for the plethora of words now of current coinage which, upon etymological inspection, prove to be the worn-out husks of what were once full-blown metaphors? Such considerations involve us in the psychology of language itself.

Muller's answer, briefly, was that in the early stages of the development of language, primitive man found his mental capacities outgrowing his vocabulary, and so pressed existing words for concrete things into service to do duty as vehicles for new, abstract meanings. Thus "spirit" is from the Latin root *spiritus,* which meant originally "wind" or "breath." Faced with the need of giving expression to a new concept of immortality, and lacking any word ready at hand, that for "wind" or "breath" was borrowed as somehow appropriate for the purpose. And, as it gained currency in its new meaning, the older meaning faded away through disuse, and it became a "fossil" or "radical" metaphor.

This theory, which achieved wide favor in its time, has by now been largely discredited, although such a distinguished authority as Sir Walter Raleigh could still base his theory of style upon Muller's system.[17] Gertrude Buck, however, brought the latest findings in child psychology to bear upon the problem and concluded that metaphors arise, not from any perception of *difference* between existing words and new concepts, but rather from *a lack of discrimination* thereof. Primitive man came to call the immortal essence "spirit" simply because he assumed that his soul and his breath were one and the same thing. It is only civilized man, fallaciously reading his own mentality back into that of the savage, who perceives such differences. For it is modern rather than ancient man whose consciousness is based upon a sharp division between the objective and subjective worlds.[18]

Miss Buck's revision of Muller's theory was echoed implicitly by J. Middleton Murry, who argued against the notion that metaphor is based upon an act of comparison (it is rather "almost a mode of apprehension"),[19] and explicitly by Owen Barfield (although he never acknowledges the fact), who coined the term "logomorphism" to describe Muller's fallacy. Barfield claims that the metaphors of modern poets are paving-stones in the road back to our long-lost mythic capacity, the primitive sense of the ultimate unity of internal and external experience.[20]

Once the theoretical point has been granted that metaphors have their source in the more primitive, undifferentiated levels of our consciousness — an assumption which in many cases has led to the brink of the symbolic approach[21] — the question still remains as to *how they function*. Herbert Spencer advanced, with his characteristic brusqueness, the rather surprising proposition that figurative is more "effective" than discursive language because it can be read with less time and effort.[22] Now, while it must be granted that figurative language is often more "vivid," universal experience attests to the fact that the reading of poetry does (and indeed should) require more time and effort than that of prose. Spencer is victimized here by a hopeless confusion between "better" and "easier."

J. G. Jennings, although starting from the healthy assumption that metaphor must be considered in its poetic contexts rather than in isolation, runs head on into two pitfalls. He claims, in the first place, that the image ("figurative object") must be truly in harmony with "the thing described," and points to Meredith's *Modern Love* as a bad example. Such criticism verges dangerously upon that passing of an act of uniformity against poets about which Coleridge warned, for discordant and rapidly shifting images are sometimes more suited to a poet's purposes — especially those of Meredith in *Modern Love* — than "harmonious" ones. He claims, secondly, that the reader must try to develop the visual aspects of metaphors in his mind's eye in order more fully to understand and appreciate poetry. But, as we have already seen, many images are not visual at all, and misbegotten attempts to visualize every image can lead only to bad reading and bad criticism.[23]

It is by now evident that the ingredients of metaphor, which Miss Buck and Owen Barfield labored so mightily to join, must be severed once more — although we must be grateful for their good work. If it be admitted that the image in a metaphor is placed in an explicitly symbolic relation, then the question must henceforth rest securely upon the relation between the "image" and the "thing imaged." Henry W. Wells, concerning himself generally with metaphor in Elizabethan literature, examines with microscopic zeal this very issue. He arrives at a series of eight categories to describe the possible range of relations between the two parts of any metaphor (he calls the thing imaged the "major term," and the image the "minor term"). The only one of his eight which has proved of any value — and here he apparently started more than he could finish — is the "radical" (not to be confused with Muller's term) or "metaphysical" image, "where two terms of a metaphor meet on a limited ground, and are otherwise definitely incongruent."[24]

Kenneth Burke became interested, among others, in this aspect of metaphor and speculated upon its function as revealing "perspective by incongruity," appealing to our insight by "exemplifying relationships between objects which our customary vocabulary has ignored."[25] Again, W. Bedell Stanford picks up the challenge thrown down by the dualists and erects it into a battle-standard. It is time, he cries, for "the psychologists and semasiologists to preach a convincing New Testament of Metaphor" based squarely upon the gospel of its essential doubleness.[26]

The work of I. A. Richards in this respect seems almost to have been written with Stanford's plea in mind. Starting with *The Meaning of Meaning,*[27] *Principles of Literary Criticism,*[28] *Practical Criticism,*[29] and continuing with *The Philosophy of Rhetoric*[30] and *Interpretation in Teaching,*[31] he has insisted upon three or four crucial points: that the image in a metaphor need not be visualized, that the prose and the poetic metaphor serve different ends and operate in correspondingly different ways, that the only test for the effectiveness of a metaphor — "mixed" or pure — is to examine its context, that the central problem lies in the relationship between the two parts of a metaphor, and that no discussion can make headway until these have been adequately named in order that we may know which of the two we are talking about at any given point. Accordingly, he suggested that we call the image the "vehicle," and the idea or thing signified via the image the "tenor" — cautioning that the total metaphor, which includes *both* tenor *and* vehicle, results in a meaning which is not to be taken as equivalent to the tenor alone, but which rather emerges from the interaction of both.

The influence which these notions have had and are still having may be seen in representative form in the work of Cleanth Brooks.[32] Arguing against traditionalist ideas of "propriety" and "decorum," he insists upon the contextual test, and avows that the meaning which emerges from the interaction of tenor and vehicle results in "a more precise sort of language than the dictionaries contain, by playing off the connotations and denotations of words against each other so as to make a total statement of a great deal more accuracy than is ordinarily attained."

Rosamond Tuve, on the other hand, takes many contemporary critical concepts to task.[33] Her motives and conclusions are remarkably similar to those of Fogle discussed above, and represent an earlier attempt to rectify the excesses of certain modern critics in their enthusiasm for "indirectness" and "concreteness." A poet like Donne, they are fond of arguing, "thinks sensuously," fusing image and idea into an "organic" whole, while a poet such as Spenser thinks and feels alternately, elaborating each in turn in a poetry which is sometimes gorgeous, sometimes philosophical, but rarely a fusion of both. Thus Donne represents a new mode of apprehension, a "shift in sensibility." The crux of Miss Tuve's defense lies in a principle she labels The Criterion of Decorum which, she argues, was understood and followed by *both* Renaissance *and* Metaphysical poets; that is, that the image must somehow be appropriate to the idea and intent of the poem. There was no shift in sensibility from Spenser to Donne, but rather a shift in genres: the Metaphysicals happened to write more exclusively in certain satirical forms which *traditionally required* an exploitation of wit, irony, indirection, and radical or non-"poetic" imagery (catachresis). Modern critics, she concludes, would do well to understand a bit more than they do of the historical situation, and to cease applying modern critical standards to the poetry of the sixteenth and seventeenth centuries.

The criterion of decorum, then, is sound criticism both past and present; but the trouble is that our modern notions of what is appropriate have undergone a sea-change. Poets of today have apparently less confidence in their ability to articulate their experience in terms of ultimate values, and so are apt to rely more heavily upon the sensory texture of their experience itself to motivate their work. Hence the modern stress upon concreteness, with its corresponding fear of "prose statement," in poetry. Neither the Renaissance nor the Metaphysical poets, Miss Tuve demonstrates, had any such compunctions.[34]

As Louis MacNeice points out, the sensory content of a poem may be either literal ("properties") or figurative ("images"), although "the properties themselves may be, in the ultimate analysis, only symbols."[35] I can see no particular reason, however, for limiting the term "imagery" to metaphor alone; the literal sensory content of a poem, by the very fact of its selection and inclusion by the poet, almost always tends to become "figurative." A given poet's preoccupation with certain settings, situations, and characters will be seen, when viewed in the perspective of his total achievement, to act as a symbolic key to his ultimate vision of life, just as his recurring metaphors, when systematically inspected, will do. In the *Iliad,* for example, the heroes and their struggles on the ringing plains of windy Troy are "imagery" as well as the shepherds, sailors, storms, and animals of the similes. (The implication is, of course, that there is a non-sensory content as well — namely discursive language. Thus a poem may contain language such as "my love is like a red, red rose," as well as "a thing of beauty is a joy forever.")

Metaphor, on the other hand, is an *explicit* means of producing symbolic imagery via figurative sensory content. Yet a poet may be bare of metaphors and still be very rich in symbolism, or he may be full of metaphors and still be lacking in any real symbolism. Indeed, it is perhaps true that most poets are liable to use a common body of images both for their literal and their figurative sensory content — tending to use the same images literally in their later work which they had employed previously in metaphors. G. Wilson Knight, for example, sees this pattern in Shakespeare's development with regard to the imagery of seas and shipwrecks.[36] Hence, it is not "metaphor" so much as "imagery" which is the essence of poetry.

Similarly, when considered under the embracing concept of symbolism, the whole vexed issue of *mental* imagery proves to have been a blind alley. Experiments have demonstrated that one can rarely equate the sensory content of one's *mind* with that of the *poem* which has been read; each of us has different image-making habits and capacities, and no two of us are likely to agree as to the sensations produced in our minds by a given line of poetry (I frequently experienced difficulty in equating Fogle's cited quotations with his argument). Furthermore, care must be taken to recognize the essential point that a figurative image in a metaphor may be sharply and vividly sensory and yet may not be *used* for its sensory qualities at all. The functioning of Eliot's famous "patient etherized upon a table" simile, describing Prufrock's evening, need depend in no way, as I read it, upon the question of whether or not either Eliot or I have reproduced in our minds the various sensations which this image is potentially capable of stimulating — the smell of the anaesthetic, the feeling of numbness, the buzzing in the ears, the pressure of the operating table upon our backs, the white and chromium gleam of the operating room, and so on. This sort of deliberate exploitation may or may not assist in grasping the symbolic import of the image, but *to understand* that this image is one of half-life, half-death, of suspended animation which is highly appropriate not only to the setting of twilight (half-light, half-dark) but also to the general theme of death-in-life in Prufrock's world upon which the poem is built, need not of necessity require any such effort. We can therefore best discuss the *functioning* of a poem's imagery without involving at any point the question of the sensations in our minds or in that of the poet.

What, then, *is* a symbol? — An image alive with an idea; a fact saturated in value. An image may become a symbol either by heredity or environment. That is to say, an image may achieve symbolic value either by virtue of its history, its relation to certain archetypal patterns appearing in myths and dreams, or by virtue of its context, its frequency of recurrence, and its relation to other images in the same work and to the author's intentions. The work done in this field may accordingly be viewed as two-fold: on the one hand we have the statisticians, and on the other the archetypalists. And, as we shall see, there is an important link between the two.

The source and fount of most current statistical studies of

poetic imagery is Caroline F. E. Spurgeon, who has often enough been criticized for what she did not do, as well as praised for what she did do.[37] Her method, well-known by now, was to sort out Shakespeare's images — *all* of them, she claimed — into various categories according to the spheres of life from which they derive. Thus we may discover from a colored chart she prepared that 15.5% of his imagery is drawn from Inanimate Nature, 13.5% from Animate Nature, 18.5% from Daily Life, and so on. She then makes the fallacious assumption,[38] completely ignoring the heredity of much clearly archetypal imagery, that these figures are the result of Shakespeare's personal experience, reflecting his personal tastes and temperament. From this she recreates a portrait of Shakespeare "the Man" that is pathetic in its naivety. She reveals here a fundamental theoretical inadequacy which is in part explained perhaps by her apparent ignorance of her predecessors. The work of Walter Whiter,[39] William Spalding,[40] Frederic Ives Carpenter,[41] T. Hilding Svartengren,[42] Edmund Blunden,[43] and F. C. Kolbe[44] would have provided useful hints and healthy correctives.

Not so naive is the second portion of her book which deals with "The Function of the Imagery as Background and Undertone in Shakespeare's Art," and which does a valuable job of interpretative criticism in actually tracing out the tone-setting recurrences in the plays.

Chief among Miss Spurgeon's followers is Una M. Ellis-Fermor, who tried the statistical method for the purpose of determining the authorship of several disputed Jacobean plays.[45] She is as uncritical in many of the same respects as was Miss Spurgeon herself.

Milton Allen Rugoff (although he claims to have begun independently) operating similarly upon the body of Donne's writings,[46] Marion Bodwell Smith upon Marlowe,[47] and Theodore Howard Banks upon Milton,[48] all offer a dreary blind alley to the hopeful student of imagery. Laboriously compiling index-files of the imagery of your favorite poet, and then composing laborious chapters from out of the file-boxes, may be virtuous work, but it is almost always endeavor in excess of the results. So Rugoff corroborates Wells's notion that Donne's metaphors are far-fetched; Miss Smith concludes that the lines which we have previously suspected were not written by Marlowe were in all probability written by someone else; and

Banks emerges with the astounding revelation that a detailed analysis of Milton's imagery bears out what we already know of his life and times.

The same theoretical inadequacy obtains here which we discovered in Spurgeon. These compilers cannot see the symbol for the images: not only are they not always certain about exactly *what* they are counting, but they are also not always certain about exactly *why*. Granted that the counting and assorting of a poet's images (literal or figurative? or both? tenor or vehicle? or both?) may be wonderfully significant, the question then arises — *of what are they significant?*

Kenneth Burke has much that is valuable to say in answer to this question, and provides a good example of how the statistical and archetypal approaches can be combined. "One cannot long discuss imagery," he comments, "without sliding into symbolism. The poet's images are organized with relation to one another [and here he has in mind Spurgeon's discovery of 'clusters,' or recurrences of similar images — or different images tending to appear together — in similar contexts] by reason of their symbolic kinships. We shift from an image of the object to its symbolism as soon as we consider it, not in itself alone, but as a function in a texture of relationships."[49] The system which he has elaborated on the basis of this concept is more complex in its applications than in its principles, and can be outlined briefly something like this: (1) the discovery of image-recurrences in the body of a poet's work gives us clues, not to his personal appearance, history, and temperament, but rather to the central conflict around which he structures his verse; (2) this conflict can be discovered by tracing out his associational clusters, or "what goes with what. . . — what kinds of acts and images and personalities and situations go with his notions of heroism, villainy, consolation, despair, etc."; and (3) the resolution or "transformation" of this conflict involves a turning *away* from one set of values (and their attendant images) and a corresponding turning *toward* another set. "So we watch, in the structural analysis of the symbolic act [the formation and transformation of a set of attitudes in a poem], not only the matter of 'what equals what,' but also the matter of 'from what to what.' "[50]

Burke developed these principles from the archetype of ritual drama, which involves at its core either a symbolic contest between Death-Evil and Life-Good, or an initiatory sloughing off (or "dying") of the childhood personality and a "rebirth" of the individual to adult rights and responsibilities. We can see, therefore, that the problem here widens from a consideration of the relation of *tenor* and *vehicle* in the single metaphor to that of *theme* and *symbol* in the whole work (although a close statistical examination of the former often provides helpful clues leading to the latter).

There are two basic sources for this archetypal approach, the one giving rise to an entire school of comparative anthropologists,[51] and the other to a line of psychological mythologists.[52] By the first is intended, of course, the monumental labor of Sir James G. Frazer, best represented by *The Golden Bough* which, in the process of probing for the roots of the puzzling priest- or king-killing rites once enacted at Nemi, wanders through a fascinating labyrinth of ritualistic parallels and often erroneous deductions thereof. Although Frazer's theories are discredited by modern anthropologists, and even his citation of parallels often questioned, there is no doubt that his work is an enormously fertile mine for students of literary symbolism. Thus, despite the contemporary anthropological stress upon the inviolable uniqueness of tribal life in any given cultural context, which may be a healthy one for anthropologists, the fact remains that certain essential patterns and images demonstrably *do* recur in ritual, myth, dream, and poem — both through time and space.[53]

The work of Carl Gustav Jung has been in large part devoted to speculations as to the source of these patterns. A practicing analytical psychologist (thus he himself distinguishes his approach from Freudian *psychoanalysis)* as well as a scholar of primitive story and custom, he is convinced that the symbolism unearthed from the dreams of his patients — most of whose difficulties stemmed from unsuccessful or incomplete attempts to assume adult responsibilities — tends to follow the patterns of myth and ritual. In other words, his patients were symbolically enacting (or trying to enact) private initiation rituals (a suggestion which is not very far from Burke's central concept of "symbolic action") in their dreams which bore an unmistakable resemblance to actual primitive initiation rites. A man who, for example, has been unable to effect a successful marital adjustment may dream that a snake is biting his penis, a phenomenon which in many ways is suggestive of the widespread circumcision rites often found to accompany the induction of young men into the tribal mysteries. Although we must leave the diagnosis of such dreams to those who know how to deal with them, we cannot deny that poems in many respects resemble dreams — although we must insist equally that they are not synonymous.

Thus Jung offers this hypothesis: myth is the "dream" of the race, dreams are the private "myths" of the individual, and poetry which manages to tap these roots of the human psyche is liable to appeal deeply and permanently to all men. The reason for this profound vitality which all sense in the work of men like Dante, Goethe, or Shakespeare is simply that they traffic continually in archetypal symbols and emotions — the ambivalence felt when one is faced with the necessity of breaking with one's parents (loss of security-revolt against authority), of taking a mate (regaining of security-loss of freedom), and of raising children (cherish-destroy).[54]

That these ambivalences appear in symbolic form in myth and legend is clearly evident: such stories as that of Sohrab and Rustum, Cupid and Psyche, and child-devouring Cronos need be mentioned only as the most patent examples. Now, not only may a poet reveal a predilection for certain of these stories (as was the case in Arnold's *Sohrab and Rustum*) but he may also use — often unconsciously — the *pattern* (motives, theme, symbols, situation, structure, etc.) of these stories in verse which is on the surface of quite a different nature. The discovery of such a pattern in such verse, Burke demonstrates, is almost sure to provide invaluable clues to its symbolic and motivational structure.

The study of Frazer and Jung and their followers soon challenges one to attempt a concise definition of these archetypal patterns. What follows, however, is to be taken not as a symbolist dictionary, the consulting of which will unlock or force any poem, but rather as a sketch of the way in which symbols have been used over the centuries and in many languages. And when we become familiar with these patterns, we make available to ourselves an interpretative technique for realizing more fully, perhaps, the possible range of emotive resonance any given image may have in a particular work.

The basic structure, then, of the archetypes is determined by the parallels which exist between the cycles of human life and those of the external world: the rising and setting of the sun, the revolution of the seasons, the waxing and waning of the moon, the circling of the stars, the ebb and flow of the tides, the growth and decay of vegetation — all these things have obviously left a profound and universal mark upon the human psyche. Thus it is quite common to speak of human things in terms of natural things: Hollywood people are "stars," old age is the "winter" of life, woman is as inconstant as the moon, one's beloved is like a flower, troubles are a "sea," and so on. Or, to take it the other way round, spring is the "birth" of the year, winter is an "old man," the sun "smiles," and so on. And just as the natural cycle has two polar phases — summer and winter, growth and decay, light and dark — so too has the human cycle — life and death, waking and sleeping, courage and fear, love and hate, striving and withdrawal.

Thus, regarding plot-structure, the archetypal pattern is three-fold: (1) birth and creation phase — imagery of childhood and paradisal gardens; (2) initiation and death phase — imagery of the journey, quest (or hunt), descent, contest, or exile (compare the witch-forest type [Hansel and Gretel, Snow White], the dragon-cave type [medieval romance], the whale-sea type [Pinocchio, Moby Dick, Jonah], and the Hades type [Homer]); and (3) rebirth phase — imagery of the return, attainment, ascent, victory, or dedicated man. It can readily be seen that this pattern coincides with the classical formula for plot-structure — conflict, crisis, resolution; complication, peripety, denouement.

The character archetypes revolve around the male-female polarity: the hero-devil-god and the woman-destroyer-preserver. Here we may expect the imagery of the wanderer, pariah, quester, or rebel (Homer's Odysseus, Milton's Satan, Joyce's Bloom); and that of the witch, mother, maid, courtezan, or enchantress (Sirens, Proserpine, Circe, Cleopatra, Dante's Beatrice).

Regarding creatures of the air, we have the dove, swallow, nightingale, swan, eagle, and lark as paradisal images; the bat and vulture as infernal images. The paradisal animals are the sheep and the lamb; the infernal are the snake, goat, and wolf; with the horse, lion, leopard (and sometimes the snake) coming somewhere in between as symbols of mysteriously creative yet potentially destructive vitality.

The imagery of setting revolves around the polarity of natural cycle. Infernal images are likely to be darkness, cold, weeds, mire, desert, and sunset-west; paradise will consist in light, warmth, flowers, mountain, garden, and sunrise-east. Fire and water are, as the imagery of man and woman, likely to be ambivalent. Fire destroys and creates, burns and refines; water is a grave and a womb, it floods and fertilizes, drowns and purifies, endangers and releases (related images are those of the whirlpool and the fountain).

Correspondingly, the archetypal theme may be stated as Illusion and Reality, with the manifold ramifications of: desire and limitation, mind and matter, permanence and flux, free-will and necessity, the individual and society, the one and the many, and so on.

Thus we have a working definition of imagery and a comprehensive frame for the interpretation of literature thereby which has the distinct advantage, it seems to me, of being built to conform to the very nature of literature itself, in that it is concerned primarily with the structure and function of symbols. A measure of the use and validity of this method is to be found in the work of such men as Northrop Frye,[55] W. H. Auden,[56] or Gaston Bachelard,[57] who bring to poetry a brilliant and wide-ranging insight, a deftness of touch, and a tact and subtlety of manner worthy of the highest ideals of scholarship and criticism.[58]

1. Reprinted from *Journal of Aesthetics and Art Criticism* 21 (1953) 25-37.

2. Caroline F. E. Spurgeon, New York and Cambridge, England, 1935.

3. Donald A. Stauffer, New York, 1949.

4. W. H. Clemen, Cambridge, Mass., 1951.

5. Edward A. Armstrong, London, 1946.

6. Wilfred Lay, The Psychological Review Monograph Supplement, No. 7, *Columbia Contributions to Philosophy, Psychology, and Education* (New York, 1898), vol. IV, no. 2.

7. Stephen S. Colvin, *The Psychological Bulletin*, VI (1909), 223-237.

8. June E. Downey, *University of Wyoming Department of Psychology Bulletin*, II (1911).

9. T. H. Pear, *British Journal of Psychology*, XIV (1924), 291-299.

10. C. W. Valentine, *British Journal of Psychology*, XIV (1923), 164-191.

56

11. See, for example, "Statistics of Mental Imagery," *Mind,* V (1880), 301-318. Galton tested for brightness, clarity, and color.

12. "The Distribution and Functions of Mental Imagery," *Teachers College, Columbia University Contributions to Education,* No. 26 (New York, 1909), pp. 87 ff.

13. *Creative Imagination: Studies in the Psychology of Literature* (New York, 1929), pp. 77-78, et passim.

14. *A Study of Poetry* (Boston and New York, 1920), pp. 74-97.

15. "Touch Images in the Poetry of Robert Browning," *PMLA,* XXXVII (1922), 574-598.

16. *The Imagery of Keats and Shelley: A Comparative Study* (Chapel Hill, 1949).

17. *Style* (New York and London, 1897), pp. 55-61.

18. "The Metaphor: A Study in the Psychology of Rhetoric," *Contributions to Rhetorical Theory,* V (Ann Arbor, 1899).

19. *The Problem of Style* (London and New York, 1925), pp. 12-13, 83-84, and 92. Cf. *John Clare and Other Studies* (London and New York, 1950), pp. 85-97.

20. *Poetic Diction: A Study in Meaning* (London, 1928), pp. 70-80, et passim.

21. Cf. Downey, *Creative Imagination,* pp. 147-148; Barfield, op. cit., pp. 79-80; Frederick Clarke Prescott, *Poetry and Myth* (New York, 1927); and Robert Graves, *Poetic Unreason and Other Studies* (London, 1925).

22. *Philosophy of Style* (New York, 1889), pp. 27-34.

23. *An Essay on Metaphor in Poetry* (London, 1915), pp. 68-82.

24. *Poetic Imagery, Illustrated from Elizabethan Literature* (New York, 1924), pp. 31, 125, 136-137, et passim.

25. *Permanence and Change: An Anatomy of Purpose* (New York, 1935), pp. 118-127.

26. *Greek Metaphor: Studies in Theory and Practice* (Oxford, 1936), p. 103, et passim.

27. With C. K. Ogden, New York and London, 1923, pp. 213 and 240.

28. New York and London, 1924, pp. 106, 119-124, and 239-241.

29. New York and London, 1929, pp. 14-15, 132, 196, 221-222.

30. New York and London, 1936, pp. 91-118.

31. New York, 1938, pp. 53-61, 87-94, 120-121. Cf. Gustaf Stern, *Meaning and Change of Meaning* (Goteborg, 1931), pp. 305-393.

32. *Modern Poetry and the Tradition* (Chapel Hill, 1939), pp. 1-17.

33. *Elizabethan and Metaphysical Imagery: Renaissance Poetic and Twentieth-Century Critics* (Chicago, 1947).

34. Cf. William Empson, "Donne and the Rhetorical Tradition," *Kenyon Review,* XI (1949), 571-587; Donald A. Stauffer, *The Nature of Poetry* (New York, 1946), pp. 128-150; and C. Day Lewis, *The Poetic Image* (London, 1947). Elizabeth Holmes, in *Aspects of Elizabethan Imagery* (Oxford, 1929), finds that the "metaphysical" image is quite characteristic of Elizabethan drama. For further works on metaphor see

also Alice Stayert Brandenburg, "The Dynamic Image in Metaphysical Poetry," *PMLA,* LVII (1942), 1039-1045; Stephen J. Brown, *The World of Imagery* (London, 1927); and Herbert Eveleth Greene, "A Grouping of Figures of Speech," *PMLA,* VIII (1983), 432-450.

35. *Modern Poetry: A Personal Essay* (Oxford, 1938), pp. 91-111.

36. Cf. *Etude sur La Metaphore* by Hedwig Konrad (Paris, 1939), pp. 146-147, et passim.

37. Cf. Una M. Ellis-Fermor, *Some Recent Research in Shakespeare's Imagery* (London, 1937); Mario Praz, *English Studies,* XVIII (1936), 177-181; Cleanth Brooks, *The Well Wrought Urn* (New York, 1947), pp. 21-46; Stanley Edgar Hyman, *The Armed Vision* (New York, 1948), pp. 209-238; Rene Wellek and Austin Warren, *Theory of Literature* (New York, 1949), pp. 215-216; G. B. Harrison, *Introducing Shakespeare,* New American Library, Mentor 14 (New York, 1947), pp. 36-40; and Kenneth Muir, "Fifty Years of Shakespeare Criticism: 1900-1950," *Shakespeare Survey 4* (1951), 1-25.

38. See Lillian Herlands Hornstein, "Analysis of Imagery: A Critique of Literary Method," *PMLA,* LVII (1942), 638-653.

39. *A Specimen of a Commentary* (London, 1794).

40. "A Letter on Shakspere's Authorship of *The Two Noble Kinsmen;* and on the Characteristics of Shakspere's Style, and the Secret of his Supremacy," *New Shakspere Society,* Series VIII, No. 1, (1876).

41. *Metaphor and Simile in the Minor Elizabethan Drama* (Chicago, 1895).

42. *Intensifying Similes in English* (Lund, 1918).

43. *Shakespeare's Significances* (London, 1929).

44. *Shakespeare's Way* (London, 1930). For an early ritualistic approach see Colin Still, *Shakespeare's Mystery Play: A Study of "The Tempest"* (London, 1921).

45. "The Imagery of *The Revengers Tragedie* and *The Atheists Tragedie,"MLR,* XXX (1935), 289-301.

46. *Donne's Imagery: A Study in Creative Sources* (New York, 1939).

47. *Marlowe's Imagery and the Marlowe Canon* (Philadelphia, 1940).

48. *Milton's Imagery* (New York, 1950).

49. *Attitudes toward History* (New York, 1937), vol. 2 of 2 vols., pp. 154-166.

50. See *The Philosophy of Literary Form: Studies in Symbolic Action* (Louisiana, 1941), pp. 20, 38-39, et passim; *A Grammar of Motives* (New York, 1945), Appendix A, et passim; and *A Rhetoric of Motives* (New York, 1950), pp. 10-13, 84-90, et passim.

51. Jane Ellen Harrison, *Themis* (Cambridge, England, 1912) and *Ancient Art and Ritual* (London and New York, 1913); Jessie L. Weston, *From Ritual to Romance* (Cambridge, England, 1920); S. H. Hooke, ed., *The Labyrinth* (London and New York, 1935); Lord Raglan, *The Hero* (London, 1936) and *Death and Rebirth* (London, 1945); Susanne K. Langer, *Philosophy in a New Key,* New American Library, Mentor 25

58

(New York, 1948 [1942]); Ernst Cassirer, *An Essay on Man* (New Haven, 1944); E. M. Butler, *The Myth of the Magus* (Cambridge, England, and New York, 1948); Bronislaw Malinowski, *Magic, Science and Religion and Other Essays* (Boston and Glencoe, Illinois, 1948); Stanley Edgar Hyman, "Myth, Ritual, and Nonsense," *Kenyon Review*, XI (1949), 455-475; Theodor H. Gaster, *Thespis: Ritual, Myth and Drama in the Ancient Near East (New York, 1950).*

52. *Maud Bodkin, Archetypal Patterns in Poetry* (London, Toronto and New York, 1948[1934]), and *Studies of Type-Images in Poetry, Religion, and Philosophy* (London, Toronto, and New York, 1951); Herbert Read, *Collected Essays in Literary Criticism* (London, 1938), pp. 101-116, and "Jung at Mid-Century," *Hudson Review,* IV (1951), 259-268; William Troy, "Thomas Mann: Myth and Reason," *Partisan Review,* V (1938), 24-32, 51-64; Mark Schorer, "Mythology (For the Study of William Blake)," *Kenyon Review,* IV (1942), 366-380; Genevieve W. Foster, "The Archetypal Imagery of T. S. Eliot," *PMLA,* LX (1945), 567-585; Joseph Campbell, *The Hero with a Thousand Faces* (New York, 1949); Philip Wheelwright, "Symbol, Metaphor, and Myth," *Sewanee Review,* LVIII (1950), 678-698, and "Notes on Mythopoeia," *Sewanee Review,* LIX (1951), 574-592; and Harry Slochower, "The Import of Myth for our Time," *trans/formation,* I (1951), 97-99.

53. For the purpose at hand, the current dispute among anthropologists as to which came first, myth or ritual, is merely an academic question.

54. For the works of Jung, see *Contributions to Analytical Psychology,* trans. H. G. and Cary F. Baynes (New York and London, 1928); *Modern Man in Search of a Soul,* trans. W. S. Dell and Cary F. Baynes (New York and London, 1933); *Psychological Types,* trans. H. Godwin Baynes (New York and London, 1923); and *Psychology of the Unconscious,* trans. Beatrice M. Hinkel (London, 1916). The work of the Freudians seems to differ chiefly in its emphasis upon the father-complex, while Jung stresses that centering about the mother. Chief among the Freudians in our field are Theodor Reik, *Ritual: Psycho-Analytic Studies,* trans. Douglas Bryan (London, 1931); Otto Rank, *The Myth of the Birth of the Hero,* trans. F. Robbins and Smith Ely Jelliffe (New York, 1914); Richard Chase, *Quest for Myth* (Baton Rouge, 1949); Erich Fromm, *The Forgotten Language* (New York and Toronto, 1951); and Thomas Mann, *Freud, Goethe, Wagner,* trans. H. T. Lowe-Porter and Rita Matthias-Reil (New York, 1939). A good contrast between the Freudian and Jungian methods at work on the same story is to be found in Mark Schorer's *The Story: A Critical Anthology* (New York, 1950), pp. 573 ff., where Edmund Wilson and Robert Heilman offer contrasting interpretations of Henry James's *The Turn of the Screw.*

55. "Blake's Treatment of the Archetype," *English Institute Essays 1950* (New York, 1951), pp. 170-196; *Fearful Symmetry: A Study of William Blake* (New Jersey, 1947); "Levels of Meaning in Literature," *Kenyon Review,* XII (1950), 246-252; "The Archetypes of Literature,"

Kenyon Review, XIII (1951), 92-110; "Yeats and the Language of Symbolism," *University of Toronto Quarterly,* XVII (1947), 1-17.

56. *The Enchafed Flood; or, The Romantic Iconography of the Sea* (New York, 1950).

57. *L'Air et les Songes* (Paris, 1943); L'Eau et les Reves (Paris, 1942); *La Terre et les Reveries de la Volonte* (Paris, 1948); *La Terre et les Reveries du Repos* (Paris, 1948).

58. The work of G. Wilson Knight should properly be mentioned here: *The Burning Oracle* (London, Toronto and New York, 1939); *The Christian Renaissance* (Toronto, 1933); *The Crown of Life* (London, Toronto and New York, 1947); *The Imperial Theme (London, 1931); Myth and Miracle* (London, 1929); *Principles of Shakespearian Production* (London, 1936); *The Shakespearian Tempest* (London, 1932); *The Starlit Dome* (London, Toronto and New York, 1941); *The Wheel of Fire* (London, 1930). Although these are often illuminating, they are too often marred by eccentricity and special pleading.

Semantics and Ontology

Philip Wheelwright

A critic may with advantage seize an occasion for trying his own conscience, and for asking himself of what real service, at any given moment, the practice of criticism either is, or may be made, to his own mind and spirit, and to the minds and spirits of others.

These words of Matthew Arnold concern criticism, and they are taken from his well-known essay, 'The Function of Criticism'; but I think they are no less relevant to an essay that purports to be, in some sense, philosophical. For philosophy, I take it, may be regarded, at least in one important perspective, as generalized and retroflective criticism — provided that criticism be understood in its best sense, as involving both an affirmative, experiential, exploratory aspect and a cautionary, analytical aspect. If 'criticism' be taken in this full and double-visioned sense, then a philosophy of criticism — or, what is perhaps the same thing, a philosophy growing out of criticism — may be conceived as both generalizing and retroflecting those double-visioned insights which it is the task of criticism to articulate. I repeat that the task of philosophy with respect to critical insights is at once to generalize and to retroflect. Philosophy will generalize such insights, in that it will seek to carry them beyond, and examine their relevance beyond, the sphere of written words and aesthetic artefacts from which criticism, in the usual literate sense of the word, sets out. Moreover, philosophy will be retroflective (a word more precise than 'reflective', now that the etymological connotations of the latter word are generally ignored) in the sense that it will turn around and look appraisingly at the postulates of method and meaning on which the critical function itself rests. It is in this sense that the present essay attempts to be philosophical: in that it will look back, however limitedly, at the assumptions of human knowledge, human articulation, and trans-human reality that underlie the full critical function.

In Bishop Berkeley's notebooks — i.e., in the compilation of jottings that was named by his earlier editor 'The Commonplace Book' and by his more recent editor Mr. A. A. Luce 'Philosophical Commentaries' — there appears the entry:

> I must not pretend to promise much of Demonstration. I must cancel all passages that look like that sort of Pride, that raising of expectation in my readers.

This is an excellent self-stricture, and virtually the same principle of limitation is reduced to an epigram by Santayana in his *Platonism and the Spiritual Life.* 'The object of spiritual discernment', Santayana writes, 'is not pure Being in its infinity, but finite being in its purity.' Of course, purity is a relative affair — especially in the City of Man, where, as Dante in *De Monarchia* says of justice, it is like a white colour all too easily soiled. But that is only to confess that lighter greys are welcome after much commerce with the darker shades.

Let us agree that every attempt at philosophical investigation starts out from some structural prejudice — some predisposition to arrange the basic categories and relations in one way rather than another. Such predisposition is unavoidable, for every attempt to avoid it falls back upon other predispositions of a more covert kind. The best thing, then, is to bring one's prejudices into the open, so far as relevant, by declaring one's main presuppositions and exposing something of the mental pattern from which one proceeds.

The main presuppositional structure that lies behind, so far as I can detect, the analysis about to be offered may be described as a basic epistemological triad in place of the epistemological dyad associated with the name of Descartes. For the Cartesian dyad of mind *vs.* matter — of mental subject *vs.* physical object — although rather widely maligned in recent critical writings, continues to cast its shadow over much of our attempted philosophical thinking. That is to say, instead of conceiving our problems in terms of the familiar subject-object dualism, I propose that we think triadically in terms of subject, object, and language; giving to language (to what Mr Richards has called the semantic 'vehicle') an equal place with the other two terms, subject and object, since neither their distinction nor their relation is possible except through linguistic operation.

Of course language, in order to take its place in this basic triadicity, must be understood in the broadest possible sense, as applying to any semantic vehicle whatever, and not as necessarily involving words and syntax. Granted that language as involving words and syntax is language of the most generally important and recognizable kind, and that for many purposes of discussion and interpretation it is advisable to employ the word 'language' in the more restricted sense, still, for basic analysis we require a broader concept — in fact, the very broadest concept possible — of that which is characterized by the unique property of referring to something other than, or at least more than, itself. Perhaps the epithet 'semantic vehicle' might seem preferable for so general a use, but there would be some danger lest both the adjective and the noun might dispose one to prejudge and limit the nature of 'that which means' and its relation to the something meant. The concept of language that my proposed analysis involves is a concept of 'that which means' in an altogether unrestricted sense. A word, a scientific formula, a poem, a ritualistic gesture, the Goldberg Variations, the Ghiberti bronze doors of the Florentine Baptistry, the falling of a leaf or of a sparrow: each such odd specimen of existence may have, for someone's mind or for some group of minds, a meaning. Each, that is to say, may not only be 'what it is and not another thing' (in Bishop Butler's forthright phrase) but may also point to, suggest, stir some inquiry about, something else — whatever the character, plausibility, and existential status of the 'something else' may be. If the letters S, L, and O are allowed to stand respectively for the subject that intends, the language whereby it intends, and the object

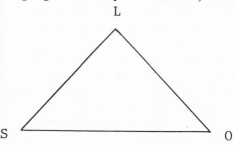

intended, then the basic structural relationship can be conveniently represented by a triangle with horizontal base, where the left apex is S, the upper apex L, and the right apex O.

Since the scheme appears to be visually the same as the well-known schematic triangle in Ogden and Richards' *The Meaning of Meaning,* let it be observed that the present analysis is quite dissociated from the main doctrine set forth in that book. In fact, it seems to me that notwithstanding Messrs Ogden and Richards' acceptance of a triadic structure and their emphasis upon the semantic, the Ogden-Richards doctrine of meaning is inadvertently too much influenced by the Cartesian dualistic epistemology, and that Mr Richards' subsequent distinction between statements and pseudo-statements is a conspicuous result of such influence. For the distinction between statements and pseudo-statements is a distinction between those statements which refer to an independent world of objects (O) and those which lack that kind of reference and merely evince an emotive and dispositional state of the subject (S). Language, then, in the earlier Ricardian doctrine, is basically subordinate to the distinction between subject and object. Although language is admittedly the indispensable vehicle by which any S can know or surmise any O, yet the function of L, according to the doctrine in question, is vehicular, not constitutive. Accordingly the essential character of L, and particularly the distinction between cognitive language and emotive language, is dependent upon the character of O and S and the relation between them. What I am proposing, on the contrary, is that we postulate a complete functional equality for S, L, and O; which is to recognize that each of the three components has a certain independence of, as well as a certain dependence upon, each of the others. For convenience of ordering let this triadic principle be called *Statement* 1. Several interesting directions of thought might suggest themselves at this point; the one that I am choosing involves an inquiry into the nature of L and its relation or relations to O.

Statement 2, then is about the nature of language. The first step, I think, should be to distinguish between block language and fluid language. By 'block' language' I mean language that ideally consists of terms defined and employed according to the law of identity, such terms being combined in such a way as to produce propositions obeying the law of non-contradiction.

This is not a complete definition of block language, but it will serve in an ordinary way to identify it. Block language can also be designated as 'literal language', or (to repeat an epithet that I have published elsewhere) 'steno-language'. Let the epithet 'fluid language', by contrast, stand for such language as has not become rigorized into block language. Two important observations have to be made about this distinction, and I shall label them 'A' and 'B'.

Statement 2A. Language may be fluid to various degrees. Block language is therefore a limiting possibility of reduced fluid language; it occurs wherever the semantic fluidity is reduced to zero while the semantic function remains. This explains why 'block language' can be defined positively whereas 'fluid language' can only be defined negatively. For it is block language that conforms to rules and hence admits of exact definition. Fluid language has an indefinite number of possibilities in an indefinite number of respects: for instance, its terms can be plurisignative, they can undergo semantic variation according to context, the meanings can be presented in soft focus and can be suggested by indirection, there can be varieties of interplay between meaning and song, the sentences can work by irony and paradox, a sentence can hover between the roles of statement and question, or between statement and exclamation, and so on.

Statement 2B. The distinction between block language, and fluid language is semantic, not ontological. It has to do with ways in which language operates — i.e., ways in which L may refer to O — and *not* with the ontological question of whether or not O has real existence. The question of whether and in what sense O exists is ontological, not semantic, and the criteria by which existence is to be judged need to be examined on their own ground. It is impossible to answer, or even to ask, except through the medium of language, the question of whether O has real existence, and we largely prejudge our answers about O by the assumptions we make about L. To some extent this is unavoidable, but the confusion should be held in check so far as possible. If L and O have a relative independence of each other (as was postulated in Statement 1), then it is necessary to keep a distinction between semantic questions regarding L and ontological questions regarding O, even though a critic needs to be alert to the varied and shifting relations between them.

Statement 3. Is there any unit of fluid discourse

corresponding to the concept (or, what is synonymous, the logical term) in block discourse? The first part of the answer is that there cannot be and should not be anything so definite. For when we employ semantic units as definite as the words 'grasshopper' or 'gravitation' or the number '3' we are *ipso facto* engaging in block discourse. But for the sake of analysis and comparison we need to be able to identify some unit or portion or aspect of fluid language which, without ceasing to be fluid, can be distinguished as having a certain character. Since the current uses of language are scarcely adequate here, we must employ the art of synecdoche and use the word 'metaphor' in a somewhat broader sense than is usual with grammarians and their pupils.

As a matter of fact the word 'metaphor' has shown itself recently capable of some semantic stretching. Particularly in certain typical critical writings of the last three decades it has tended to take on a different meaning, or at least a different emphasis, from the traditional one. The traditional meaning of 'metaphor' receives its classical definition in the *Poetics,* where Aristotle writes: 'Metaphor (*metaphora*) is the transference (epiphora) of a name [from that which it usually denotes] to some other object.' Although the phrase 'from that which it usually denotes' is justified by the context rather than by any corresponding set of Greek words, yet the idea which the phrase conveys is traditionally an essential part of the usual idea of metaphor from Aristotle onwards. Quintilian and a host of later grammarians have said virtually the same thing, and what they have said can be analysed into three propositions: (1) that a word which is used metaphorically has some usual and familiar meaning to begin with; (2) that in a given instance the word is made to stand for some other meaning which is less usual or less familiar or more vague; and (3) that the justifying bond between the usual meaning of the word and the present 'metaphoric' meaning is some kind of similarity. The first two of these propositions are expressed in the sentence just quoted from Chapter 22 of the *Poetics;* the third proposition is expressed in another sentence in the same chapter, where Aristotle writes: 'A good metaphor implies an intuitive perception of the similarity of dissimilars.' Virtually the same view of metaphor is expressed in the late J. Middleton Murry's statement that metaphor is 'the means by which the less familiar is assimilated to the more familiar'.

By contrast consider the definition of 'metaphor' offered by Sir Herbert Read in his *English Prose Style:* 'Metaphor is the synthesis of several units of observation into one commanding image; it is the expression of a complex idea, not by analysis, nor by abstract statement, but by a sudden perception of an objective relation.' The main idea that is expressed in Sir Herbert's definition is evidently quite different from the usual idea of metaphor. For whereas metaphor in the usual sense operates by resemblance between something familiar and something unfamiliar, the trope referred to in the new definition consists rather of a grouping of several dissimilars and a relating them on the basis of a felt congruity. In order to distinguish more conveniently the two kinds of metaphor I shall employ the words 'epiphor' and 'diaphor'. The word 'epiphor' is a transliteration of Aristotle's own word, *epiphora,* by which he describes metaphor, and which is usually translated 'transference'. The word 'diaphor', although not quite a new word (having been employed by Friedrich Max Muller in a somewhat different sense), is newly suggested for the present purpose. Its use here is justified by its etymology, or rather by the parallel etymologies of the two contrasting words. For whereas 'epiphor' connotes a semantic movement (*phora*) from something on to (*epi-*) something else, the word 'diaphor' connotes a semantic movement through (*dia-*) a grouping of several particulars. The point of my fourth Statement is not merely a contrast of definitions but also the judgment that in any good metaphor there is some combination, in whatever degree, of epiphoric and diaphoric ingredients. In a metaphor, as Paul Henle has pointed out,[2] there are likely to be two kinds of resemblance involved: an antecedent resemblance, which justifies the metaphoric comparison in the first place, and an induced resemblance, which arises from the very fact that a comparison has been made. Professor Henle's pair of words is both relevant and useful, and I would suggest that a metaphor is perhaps epiphoric to the extent that an antecedent resemblance is effective, diaphoric to the extent that the significant resemblance is that which has been induced by, and is emergent from, the metaphor itself.

Statement 4. The relation of metaphor to symbol. The use of the two words 'metaphor' and 'symbol' has been so varied as to produce a confused situation. The confusion can be illustrated by the different word-uses employed in two books — Wilbur M.

Urban's *Language and Reality* and Martin Foss's *Metaphor and Reality*. Urban, who presumably follows Coleridge in this regard, distinguishes the two terms by saying that a metaphor can be adequately paraphrased, whereas a symbol cannot. Foss, on the contrary, takes 'symbol' to mean a piece of what I have called block language — the word 'grasshopper' and the number '3' would be typical symbols for him — and contrasts it with 'metaphor', which is a unique expression of meaning, *sui generis* and irreducible. In short, these two writers, the late Professor Urban and Professor Foss, employ the pair of words in almost mutually reversed senses. Foss takes the word 'symbol' as it is taken in mathematics and in those schools of logic which model their methods after mathematical procedures; Urban takes the word as it is taken notably by Mallarmé and the French *symbolistes*. So egregious a confusion needs clearing up; and while perfect clarity cannot be expected in so metamorphic a situation, I should like to explore the possibilities of clarity along the following lines.

Let us continue to take 'metaphor' in the way that has been outlined in the previous section of the argument — as involving both epiphoric and diaphoric components. I would suggest that a metaphor is untranslatable to the extent of, and because of, its diaphoric component. But while the diaphoric component does introduce an element of irreducible novelty when it is first composed, yet its novelty wears off as time flows on, and it may eventually, if used too much, become a piece of literal language or a cliche. For example, the word 'skyscraper' was originally a metaphor. Its epiphoric component consisted in the implicit analogy which gave logical justification to the invention of the word; its diaphoric component consisted in the novelty, amounting almost to a paradox, of combining the idea of sky with the mundane idea of scraping. (I can personally recall the diaphoric quality which the word 'skyscraper' had for me when as a small boy I was taken to New York and heard the word for the first time as the then imposing Flatiron Building was pointed out to me.) On a more consciously organized level the epithet 'waste land' had both epiphoric and diaphoric aspects — epiphoric relevance and diaphoric vitality — when Mr. Eliot published it as a title; and it can still have both qualities for those who can attend to what the poem says as distinguished from what a thousand critics and journalists have said about it — a very hard line to draw, incidentally. But in the forty years since its distinguished inception the epithet has, in many quarters, degenerated into a stereotype, readily available to leader writers, Class Day orators, and other public moralists. The history of language offers countless other illustrations of how a metaphor, originally combining a recognizable comparison with a stimulating freshness of synthesis, gradually settles into the respectability of literalness, becoming a unit of block language. One may speculate, in a moments's wonder, upon the connotative differences between a modern philosopher declaring securely, 'I exist', and an early Indo-European, whose language permitted him only the sentence 'I breathe', dimly apprehending something of its transcendental suggestiveness.

Returning to the word 'symbol' I would suggest that a symbol may be regarded as a metaphor stabilized, and then would further suggest that the stabilization may occur in either of two ways. The original diaphoric diversity may become neutralized and forgotten, so that the original point of the epiphor is lost also (as in two instances just cited): in which case the result is a steno-symbol, a block symbol. On the other hand the original diaphoric diversity and quality may be retained and enriched on subsequent occasions when the metaphor is contemplated: in which case the result is a tensive symbol. Professor Foss means by 'symbol' a block symbol, whereas Coleridge, Professor Urban, and the French *symbolistes* mean by 'symbol' a tensive symbol. Block symbols are what logical positivists assume to be the ultimate ingredients of meaning; at least it is assumed, I think, that in a logico-mathematical heaven a universal reduction of all meanings to clear-cut terms and relations will be possible. On the other hand, tensive symbols are what interest us as critics and humanists. Let us recognize that they are not reducible to block symbols; that they have a metamorphic, indefinitely extensible, and always somewhat problematical character; and that they are the living marrow of thought, as distinguished from its encased skeletons.

Statement 5. My paper concludes with a question; and I fear that neither time nor the present stage of my own thinking permits me to go much beyond a formulation of the question and one or two emergent suggestions. In broadest terms the question has to do with the relation of tensive language to reality. Although I cannot offer an adequate answer, and indeed would be suspicious of any answer that claimed adequacy, I should like to introduce three terms into the discussion and offer a few observations as to their interrelations and their relevance to the inquiry. The first term is *imagination* — that is, what Coleridge means by 'secondary imagination'. It is to be discussed, I believe in one or more of the papers that follow. Secondly there is the Platonic - Aristotelian word *mimesis,* which is usually translated 'imitation', although there are contexts in which 'representation' might do more accurate service. Thirdly there is the Platonic word *methexis,* 'participation'. The term 'mimesis' can be the most readily clarified of the three, I think, and then the relation of it to the others can be better seen.

In the *Poetics* the word 'mimesis' is employed rather inadequately. There Aristotle confuses the matter by putting too much emphasis upon the simple kind of visual imitation that enables someone to exclaim, he says, 'Ah, that is so-and-so!' when looking at a painting. Elsewhere in the *Poetics* a more mature concept of *mimesis* is offered when Aristotle speaks of a dramatic plot as 'imitating' a certain kind of action. But the *Poetics* needs to be supplemented, with respect to this problem, by certain quotations from other Aristotelian writings. In particular there are two. In the *Physics* Aristotle writes:

Art either imitates nature or else gives the finishing touches to what nature has left incomplete.

And in the *Metaphysics* he writes:

Imperishable forms are imitated by things in a natural condition of change.

The first of these two quotations has an interestingly metabiological look. Aristotle, whose ultimate orientation is always biological rather than either inertly physical or super-worldly, is regarding the artist as one who not merely repeats what nature has accomplished but also carries on where nature has left off. I would suggest that his statement could be improved by putting 'both and' in place of 'either or'; for in art there is both an element of the imitative and an element of the creative. Accordingly I should prefer to modify Aristotle's statement in the *Physics* to read as follows:

Art both in some sense imitates nature and also gives the finishing touches to what nature has left incomplete.

The second quotation, the one from the *Metaphysics,* is more Platonic in character, and it naturally suggests the question: In what sense, precisely, can particular things in the changing world be said to imitate imperishable forms? Or, coming closer to our subject: In what sense can an artist, while practising his art in some concrete fashion, be said to imitate imperishable forms?

A clue might be found, it seems to me, by distinguishing and comparing two ways in which a primitive artist might imitate a totemic animal, say a deer. He might mime the deer by dancing, and he might make a drawing of the deer on the wall of a cave. Now it is generally agreed by anthropologists that a totem was never a single animal but was an entire species. The deer as a universal type was the object to be ceremonially danced and painted. But it was not merely a type, it was nothing so definite as a universal in the logician's sense; it was a *presence.* The ceremonial dancer was expressing the grace and agility of the deer, and no doubt other qualities which, although they cannot be caught in the net of verbal language, we may suppose were inarticulately present in his awareness. Moreover he felt himself to be participating in those qualities; in expressing the deer's nimbleness he was imaginatively and kinaesthetically identifying himself with it; there was miming and participating at the same time — an effective collusion of *mimesis* and *methexis.*

Now consider the other main kind of primitive imitation — the painting of a deer on a cave wall. The caves of the Aurignacian period in France and . Spain were presumably dedicated to religious practices, as Miss Gertrude Levy in *The Gate of Horn* has convincingly argued. Hence the drawings would have been made in a spirit of devotion. Moreover, as Miss Levy has observed, there is significance in the fact that an animal is sometimes drawn where there is already a depression in the rock to serve as its head or a branching pair of fissures to serve as its antlers. The artist who made such use of natural configurations was unconsciously exemplifying Aristotle's phrase; he gave 'finishing touches to what nature has left incomplete'. Miss Levy suggests that the Aurignacian artist, seeing an unfinished head or pair of horns in the configurations of the rock, may have felt the totemic animal's presence there, struggling, as it were, to come forth. On that hypothesis the Aurignacian artist's activity would have been not only imitative of the animal shapes he knew, but also darkly participative in the spirit of the forthcoming new animal life. Thus what I am suggesting is that an Aurignacian may have found it natural to combine imitation and participation both in painting and in the dance.

Any conclusive proposition would be inadequate to so large and inviting a subject. I shall not offer one, except of a problematical and open kind. It seems to me that some most interesting discussions might be pursued concerning the interrelated roles of imagination, imitation, and participation; and that along such paths occasional glimpses might be enjoyed of that cloud-covered landscape which we call the Relation of Art to Reality.

1. Reprinted from *Metaphor and Symbol* L. C. Knights and Basil Cottle, eds. London: Butterworths Scientific Publications 1960 pp. 1-9.

2. Paul Henle, 'Metaphor', in *Language, Thought, and Culture,* edited by Paul Henle (University of Michigan Press, 1958).

The Metaphorical Twist

Monroe C. Beardsley

Of all the questions about metaphor that interest the literary theorist or philosophic aesthetician, the foremost — that is, first and fundamental — one is, of course: what is it? To give an adequate account of metaphor as linguistic phenomenon, on which to base our account of it as poetic phenomenon, is to say what is peculiar to metaphorical expressions, how they differ from literal ones, how we recognize them and know what they mean.

It is not easy to say exactly what are the issues over this problem. There are several ways of describing metaphor, some of them going back to ancient times, that are so familiar and so confidently echoed from one writer to another that they all have the air of being roughly equivalent. But there is, I believe, an important distinction among them, and part of my purpose here is to drive a wedge — to separate things out more sharply than has been done. I want to distinguish what might be called a thing-approach and a word-approach to the problem of analyzing metaphor.

According to one of these views, taken broadly, the modifier (as I call it) in the metaphor — for example, the word "spiteful" in "the spiteful sun" — retains its standard designative role when it enters into the metaphor and therefore continues in that context to denote the same objects it denotes in literal contexts. Thus the metaphor is an implicit comparison, an elliptical simile, and says in effect that the sun is like a spiteful person. The spiteful person is referred to, in this context, just as is the sun — there are two objects. The metaphor, as Johnson said, "gives you two ideas instead of one." Mr. John Crowe Ransom has classified metaphors as "Importers" that introduce "foreign objects" into the "situation"[2]) — I guess he was thinking of those fancy importers of exotic foodstuffs, like truffles and candied bees. The metaphor, in his view, drags an alien and uncalled-for object into the context (delighting us, the Eighteenth Century theorist might say, by its charm and novelty), and thereby adds to that "local texture of irrelevance" that Ransom considers so essential to poetry.

Let us call this the Object-comparison Theory of metaphor. According to its rival, the Verbal-opposition Theory, no such importation or comparison occurs at all, but instead a special feat of language, or verbal play, involving two levels of meaning in the modifier itself. When a predicate is metaphorically adjoined to a subject, the predicate loses it ordinary extension, because it acquires a new intension — perhaps one that it has in no other context. And this twist of meaning is forced by inherent tensions, or oppositions, within the metaphor itself.

I propose to give reasons for rejecting the Object-comparison Theory, both in its general form and in a special form that has recently been offered. Then I shall explain more fully the Verbal-opposition Theory, and defend it against some possible objections.

I

Now up to a point, I admit, it does not matter whether you talk of metaphors in the object-fashion or in the semantical fashion. But only up to a point. Thus suppose the word "briar" is introduced metaphorically into a certain context, as, say, in "East Coker" — the reference to

> frigid purgatorial fires
> Of which the flame is roses, and the smoke is briars.[3]

You can start your explication either in object-language (talking about the characteristics of briars) or in metalanguage (talking about the connotations of the *word* "briars"). You can say, "Briars have the capacity to scratch people, to retard their progress, to be made into pipes," and so on. Or you can say, "The word 'briars' connotes such properties as being scratchy, retarding progress, being made into pipes," and so on. But though these two ways of speaking overlap, since in part the connotations of the *word* derive from what is generally true of the *objects,* they do not coincide completely.

For the connotations are controlled not only by the properties the object actually has but by those it is widely *believed* to have — even if the belief is false. This is my first argument against the Object-comparison Theory, then — that a consistent adherence to that theory would produce incorrect or incomplete explications of metaphors in cases where the modifier has connotations, applicable in that context, that are not common accidental features of the objects denoted. For example, some of the important marginal meaning of "briars" in the Eliot poem comes, of course, from the way the crown of thorns figures in the Christian story. And quite apart from its historical truth, the existence of that religion is sufficient to give the word that meaning. If in explicating this line we limit ourselves to what we know about briars, we would not fully understand it.

My second argument against the Object-comparison Theory is that once we commit ourselves to finding, or supplying, an object to be compared with the subject of the metaphor (that is, in I. A. Richards' terms, a "vehicle" to make it go) we open the way for that flow of idiosyncratic imagery that is one of the serious barriers between a reader and a poem. Consider an example also discussed by Mr. Ransom, the lines about Brutus's sword in Anthony's speech:

Mark how the blood of Caesar follow'd it,
As rushing out of doors, to be resolv'd
If Brutus so unkindly knock'd or no

(III, ii, 178). Ransom speaks of the "shift" from the tenor (the blood) to a "page" opening the door, the page being the vehicle.[4] Now there is obviously no page in these lines, any more than there is a rudely-awakened householder or soon-to-be-embattled farmer alarmed by Paul Revere. Where does the page come from? The tenor-vehicle terminology, with its underlying assumption that the metaphor must be a comparison, tempts the explicator to invent, where he cannot discover, a vehicle; and so we get the page. But "rushing out of doors" is not exactly synonymous with "page rushing out of doors," as applied to Caesar's blood. And it is the first meaning that the explicator is to keep his eye on, not the further meaning imported — a good description — by his own fancy.

Quoting a characteristic metaphor of Samuel Johnson's, "Time is, of all modes of existence, most obsequious to the imagination," William K. Wimsatt, Jr., remarks, "We need not imagine Time as a butler bowing to his master the Imagination."[5]

My third argument against the Object-comparison Theory is that it tends to lead to the unfortunate doctrine of "appropriateness." If a metaphor is a comparison, it is possible to ask whether the comparison is "apt" or "farfetched." We see this in Aristotle's fourth type of bad taste, his objection to the phrase of Gorgias, "events that are fresh and full of blood."[6] If we take Macbeth's words, (II, iii),

> their daggers
> Unmannerly breech'd with gore

to be comparing bloody daggers and breeched legs, and if we inquire into its appropriateness, we are likely to say, like the Nineteenth Century critic quoted by Cleanth Brooks,[7] that Shakespeare "disgusts us with the attempted comparison." But the correct question is what is *meant* by the words — what properties are attributed to the daggers via the marginal meanings of the metaphorical attribute. It is of no moment whether bloody daggers in general are best so described; the question is what we learn from this description about *these* daggers, and their role in the whole story — or about the speaker who describes them this way.

To put the point more generally: Suppose the poet remarks, "My sweetheart is my Schopenhauer." On the Comparison Theory we are to ask what his sweetheart and Schopenhauer have in common. But we don't *know* his sweetheart, so how can we answer this question until he tells us, by the metaphor itself, what she is like? The correct question is what possible meanings of "Schopenhauer" can apply to the sweetheart, and are not ruled out by the context.

II

My general objections to the Object-comparison Theory apply, I believe, with like force to the very interesting form of this theory that has been advanced by Paul Henle: the Iconic Signification Theory.[8] Mr. Henle actually seems to hold both of the theories that I have named. His version of the Verbal-opposition Theory, however, is described in terms of the reader's response — his "shock" at the "clash of meanings."[9] I prefer to state the theory as a theory, not about the effect of metaphor, but about the linguistic structure that causes the effect — about the "clash" of meanings" itself. Mr. Henle says little about this, and he does not explain its relation to his other, and main, theory — indeed, he does not say why there should be any shock, or any clash, if the other is correct.

Mr. Henle holds that "there is an iconic element in metaphor," and he proposes to analyze metaphorical attributions in terms of the concept of iconic signs. In his example from Keats, "hateful thoughts enwrap my soul in gloom," he says there are two relationships: first, the word "enwrap" designates a certain action — "envelopment in a cloak." Second, this action is made an iconic sign of gloom.[10] "In a metaphor, some terms symbolize the icon and others symbolize what is iconized."[11]

We might begin by asking how the cloak gets into this explication. The Iconic Theory seems to import an alien object of some sort — like Mr. Ransom's page — and it is subject to the difficulties in the theory of importation. Mr. Henle has even yielded to the "appropriateness" doctrine, which, as I suggested, the Comparison Theory at least makes tempting. Thus he says that "it would not have done to speak of hateful thoughts *entrapping* the soul in gloom," because traps "are all sharp, with definite edges, and this spoils the correspondence with gloom."[12] Perhaps I should not put so much stress on this remark, but I must say that it would generalize into a most astonishing critical principle. For my part, I think the question whether wraps or traps are better iconic signs of gloom is a wholly unanswerable question, and fortunately it does not need to be asked. If the speaker in the poem had been trapped in gloom, rather than wrapped in it, that would simply have said something different about him, and about how he felt, and came to feel that way — which might have made a worse poem, or a better one, depending on several other things.

Mr. Henle cites one of Aristotle's examples of the way in which "proportional analogies" can be inverted: another is that we can say either that the shield is the bowl of Ares or the bowl is the shield of Dionysus.[13] "That such inversion is possible is of course a consequence of the iconic character of metaphor," says Mr. Henle.[14] And maybe it does follow from any Object-comparison Theory, for if A can be compared to B, why not B to A? And a statement of likeness is equivalent to its own converse. But if it follows, that is a fatal objection to the theory. Now Mr. Henle realizes that there is a difficulty, and so he says that though metaphors are always reversible, sometimes the "feeling tone is different." I don't believe this will do: the difference between "this man is a lion" and "that lion is a man"[15] is in what the different metaphorical modifiers attribute to the two subjects. In the Verbal-opposition Theory, it does not follow that because A's are metaphorically B's, therefore B's are metaphorically A's. That is just the difference between a metaphor and Aristotle's proportional analogy, or relational simile — even if Aristotle himself thought the difference was not great. And surely the Verbal-opposition Theory is correct in this consequence, while the Iconic Theory, if it entails that in calling men lions and lions men we are in both cases attributing the same properties, is clearly false.

One other objection can, I think, be fairly made against the Iconic Signification Theory. It should be counted as a merit in a theory of metaphor that it can analyze metaphor in the same terms that will do for oxymoron. This makes for economy of theory, and it fits in with the evidently deep affinities between these two types of expression. Now the Iconic Theory is somewhat handicapped here, for it does not seem to work well for oxymoron. In "mute cry" (if that may be taken as an example), we should have to say that a mute person was being made an iconic sign of something that is not mute: soundlessness becomes a sign of sound. This is not very convincing. The truth seems rather to be that in oxymoron we have the archetype, the most apparent and intense form, of verbal opposition.

III

If we turn from the objects referred to in the metaphor, and consider the significations of the words themselves, we must look for the metaphoricalness of the metaphor, so to speak, in some sort of conflict that is absent from literal expressions. One direction in which this conflict has been searched for may, I think, be quickly marked off as a dead end. This approach contrasts the meaning of the expression itself and the idea in the speaker's (or writer's) mind. To call A a B metaphorically, in this view, is to say that A is a B without meaning it — metaphor is a form of irony.[16] The implicit appeal here is to intention, and the theory suffers from all the ills associated with that notion. We do not decide that a word in a poem is used metaphorically because we know what the poet was thinking; rather we know what he was thinking because we see that the word is used metaphorically. The clues to this fact must somehow be in the poem itself, or we should seldom be able to read poetry.

There is a hint of a similar view in the excellent account of metaphor in Isabel Hungerland's recent book.[17] In the metaphor, she says, "There must be some ascertainable point in the deviation from or violation of ordinary usage — another way of putting it is that the violation must be deliberate." Mrs. Hungerland has since said that the second clause here was inadvertent; I mention it only to emphasize that the two clauses are surely far from equivalent, because accidental or unintended metaphors are perfectly possible.[18]

The opposition that renders an expression metaphorical is, then, within the meaning-structure itself. The central features of such a Verbal-opposition Theory I have already expounded elsewhere,[19] but I should like to recapitulate them briefly here. In that version, I said that the possibility of the metaphorical performance — the opportunities that a living language presents for fooling around with meanings in this particular way — depend upon a felt difference between two sets of properties in the intension, or signification, of a general term: first, those properties that (at least in a given sort of context) are taken to be necessary conditions for applying the term correctly in a particular sense (these are the defining, or designated, properties, or the central meaning of the term in that sort of context); second, those properties that belong to the marginal meaning of the term, or (in the literary critic's sense of the word) its connotation — properties that a speaker can, in appropriate contexts, show that he attributes to an object by using that term without claiming to follow a rule that he would not apply the term to that kind of object if it did not have that property. I said that when a term is combined with others in such a way that there would be a logical opposition between its central meaning and that of the other terms, there occurs that shift from central to marginal meaning which shows us the word is to be taken in a metaphorical way. It is the only way it can be taken without absurdity. The term "logical opposition" here includes both direct incompatibility of designated properties and a more indirect incompatibility between the presuppositions of the terms — as when our concept of the sun rules out the possibility of voluntary behavior that is presupposed by the term "spiteful." The logical opposition is what gives the modifier its metaphorical twist.

A metaphorical attribution, then, involves two ingredients: a semantical distinction between two levels of meaning, and a logical opposition at one level. Thus there is no question of "spiteful," in a metaphorical context, denoting spiteful people and injecting them for the purpose of comparison; the price it pays for admission to this context is that it function there to signify only its connoted characteristics.

Such is the Simple Verbal-opposition Theory as I have defended it, and it seems to me to be right up to a point. That is, I believe that the phenomenon it describes, the shift from designation to connotation, actually occurs. But I am afraid it is not enough. Something else that is very important also happens in at least some metaphors, I now think.[20] And to explain it, we must make (or make more explicit than was done in the earlier version) two distinctions.

The connotations of a word standing for objects of a certain kind, it will be agreed, are drawn from the total set of accidental properties either found in or attributed to such objects. Let us call this set of accidental properties the *potential range of connotation* of that word. At a given time in the history of the word, however, not all of these properties will perhaps have been made use of. Thus, think of a number of properties characteristic of trees, though not necessarily present in all: leafiness, shadiness, branchiness, tallness, slimness, having bark, suppleness in the wind, strength, and so on. Some of these, such as leafiness, shadiness, tallness, clearly belong among the recognized connotations of "tree," readily called into play in familiar metaphors. They may be called *staple connotations.* Other properties, such as perhaps slimness and having bark, do not seem to be staple connotations, though they may be sufficiently characteristic of trees to be available in the potential range of connotation. They may wait, so to speak, lurking in the nature of things, for actualization — wait to be captured by the word "tree" as part of its meaning in some future context.

My first distinction, then, is between two sets of accidental properties — not a sharp distinction, not one that can always be cut with confidence, but still objectively determinable. My second distinction is between two kinds of metaphor — and it is subject to similar qualifications.

Suppose we begin by trying to divide metaphors into two classes. Let us try putting into Class I metaphors like "smiling sun" and "the moon peeping from behind a cloud." Note that these are not dead metaphors — that is not the problem involved here. They are live, but somehow they are different from those we might put into Class II: "the spiteful sun," "unruly sun," "faithful sun," "inconstant moon." We recognize, it seems safe to say, that those in Class II are more interesting than those in Class I — which is not, of course, to say that they are better in every poetic context. But what is the difference?

Now, in terms of the Simple Verbal-opposition Theory, something can be said by way of explanation. The Class II metaphors are more complex than the Class I metaphors. They seem to say more about the object. They are thus more precise, more discriminating, as descriptions. To speak of the sun as "smiling" is to imply a broad contrast with a sun that does not succeed in smiling, perhaps, or that is angry and beats down on the desert.

But to speak of the sun as "unruly" is to imply a sharper distinction between this quality and other qualities conceived with comparable specificity: obedience, punctuality, deference to one's wishes. Now the Verbal-opposition Theory, even in its simple form, allows degrees of complexity, and so perhaps it can at least partly explain the difference between the two classes. Yet there seems to be more to the matter even than this.

It is at this point that we encounter a very tricky question indeed. For one suggestion that seems obvious enough is this: the Class I metaphors are trite and banal; the Class II metaphors are fresh and novel. If there is truth in this description, it can only be won and kept by skillful maneuvering around some deceptive shoals. In the first place, we must not, I think, suppose that it is a matter of mere repetition. Perhaps "smiling sun" has been said more often than "inconstant moon," but even if we were to repeat the phrase from *Romeo and Juliet* over and over until we were tired of it, and therefore were in no position to attend to its meaning, that would not alone make it trite. In any case, if triteness is a frequency-notion, then it is not what makes the difference here. Yet in the second place, the nature of a particular metaphor cannot be entirely independent of its date in the history of English literature. For what it does mean, or can mean, at a given time must depend to some extent on what other contexts the words have appeared in, and what analogous or parallel expressions exist in the language.

IV

Let us suppose that when the metaphor "th'inconstant moon" is first constructed in English, it is the first time that "inconstant" has been used metaphorically – or at least the first time it has been applied to an inanimate object. (This, of course, does not preclude the possibility that it may originally have applied *only* to inanimate objects, say, to their rotational motion; if at some time it came to have the psychological or behavioral meaning as its primary one, then we can speak of the first metaphorical use after this time). At this moment the word "inconstant" *has* no connotations. When, therefore, we find "inconstant moon," we seize upon the verbal opposition, all right, but when we look for relevant connotations we are balked. How, then, can we explicate it? Given the surrounding syntax and the prevailing tone, it claims to make sense; therefore we must try to make it make sense. And so we look about among the accidental or contingent properties of inconstant people in general, and attribute these properties, or as many of them as we can, to the moon. And these properties would, for the moment at least, become part of the meaning of "inconstant," though previously they were only properties of those people. Then we might say that the metaphor transforms a *property* (actual or attributed) into a *sense.* And if, taking their lead from this license, other poets were to find other metaphorical applications for "inconstant," which employed the same properties and created similar, or overlapping, senses, then those senses might become closely enough connected with the word so that they would be relatively fixed as connotations of that word. In this way the metaphors would not only actualize a potential connotation, but establish it as a staple one.

Here is where the Object-comparison Theory makes its contribution after all. For it is correct in saying that sometimes in explicating metaphors we must consider the properties of the objects denoted by the modifier. But those objects are not referred to for comparison: they are referred to so that some of their relevant properties can be given a new status as elements of verbal meaning.

Let us suppose that at a given time in the history of the English language we have already in existence such metaphors as "smiling sky," "smiling sea," and "smiling garden." The modifier cannot, of course, mean exactly the same thing in all these contexts, but there will be some meaning in common. And let us suppose this common meaning is already established as the connotation of "smiling." When a poet for the first time speaks of a "smiling sun," what will happen? The logical opposition is plain, so we turn first to the staple connotations of "smiling" and apply them to the sun (as the simple Verbal-opposition Theory says). But we go no further. Perhaps we cannot go further; perhaps we are just not forced to. In any case, we see that it is a metaphor, and we can read it correctly, but we do not take it as *creating* meaning in the same way as Class II metaphors. It is merely borrowing its sense, relying on what is already established and available.

The Revised Theory can be well illustrated by a very interesting metaphor that I have borrowed from Paul Henle. In one of his devotional works, Jeremy Taylor says that "Chaste marriages are honourable and pleasing to God," that widowhood can be "amiable and comely when it is adorned. with gravity and purity," but that "virginity is a life of angels, the enamel of the soul . . ."[21] This was not the earliest metaphorical use of "enamel;" we learn from the NED that Donne, in 1631, had already used the phrase "enameled with that beautiful Doctrine of good Workes," and that Evelyn, in 1670, had used the phrase "enamel their characters." Moreover, Taylor himself, in the dedication to his *Sermons,* spoke of "those truths which are the enamel and beauty of our churches." Perhaps such usages had already established some of the properties of enamel as staple connotations of the word; perhaps not. We would have to know this in order to know exactly how definitely in Class II was the metaphor "the enamel of the soul" in the context of Taylor's *Of Holy Living.* But of our own time we can make a surer judgment. Enamel is hard, resistant to shock and scrape, applied with labor and skill, and decorative. I should think some of these are not fully established as recognized connotations of the word. Yet to speak of virginity as the enamel of the soul is surely to say (as Mr. Henle points out) that it is a protection for the soul, and that it is the final touch of adornment on what is already well-made. Thus this metaphor does not merely thrust latent connotations into the foreground of meaning, but brings into play some properties that were not previously meant by it.

It seems to me that we probably have to distinguish at least three stages in this metamorphosis of verbal meaning, even though the points of transition are not clearly marked. In the first stage we have a word and properties that are definitely not part of the intension of that word. Some of those properties are eligible to become part of the intension, to join the range of connotation. In order to be eligible, they have to be fairly common (actual or imputed) properties, typical properties — not just in the statistical sense, but normally or characteristically present in the objects denoted by the word. Thus, for example, suppose someone said that whiteness could become a connotation of "enamel." This could happen, I should think, if most or all enamel were white, or if enamel were usually white except when affected by external conditions, or if the best enamel were white, or if the whitest white things were enamelled things.

When the word comes to be used metaphorically in a certain sort of context, then what was previously only a property is made, at least temporarily, into a meaning. And widespread familiarity with that metaphor, or similar ones, can fix the property as an established part of the meaning. It is still, in this second stage, not a necessary condition for applying the word. Even if "tree" connotes tallness, there is no contradiction in speaking of a short or stunted tree. Still, if someone said that his tree was a tree "in the fullest sense" (compare "He is in every sense a man,)" we should, I think, be justified in taking him to be saying, among other things, that it had reached a good height, at least for its species.

When a connotation becomes so standardized for certain types of context, it may be shifted to a new status, where it becomes a necessary condition for applying the word in that context. It then constitutes a new standard sense. This third stage is illustrated by the dead metaphor: "tail," used in connection with automobile lights, now owes nothing to animal tails, and its meaning can be learned by someone who never heard that animals had tails. Not all connotations, of course, pass into this third stage, but some are always doing so.

Perhaps some portion of this history can be traced in words like "warm" and "hard" that are taken over from the sensory realm and applied to human personality — as apparently happens in many languages.[22] I should think that the first application of "warm" to a person had to change some accidental properties of warm things into part of a new meaning of the word, though now we easily think of these properties as connotations of "warm" — for example, approachable, pleasureable-in-acquaintance, inviting. These qualities were part of the potential range of connotation of "warm" even before they were noted in warm things, which may not have been until they were noted in people and until someone, casting about for a word that would metaphorically describe those people, hit upon the word "warm." But before those qualities could come to belong to the staple connotation of "warm," it had to be discovered that they could be *meant* by the word when used in an appropriate metaphor. Finally, although it has not happened yet, "warm person" may come to lose its metaphorical character, with the present connotations of "warm" changing into a new designation. It would then be a dead metaphor.

If the Revised Verbal-opposition Theory is correct, it would account for a good deal. It does better than the simple theory at explaining the remarkable extent to which metaphor can expand our verbal repertoire beyond the resources of literal language.[23] It allows for novelty, for change of meaning, even for radical change. It admits the unpredictability of metaphor, the surprising ideas that may emerge even from chance juxtapositions of words. It shows that a metaphor can be objectively explicated, for the properties of things and the connotations of words are publicly discoverable, and disputes about them are in principle resolvable. And it explains the comparative obscurity, or momentary puzzlingness, of the Class II metaphor, which may take time to understand completely.

V

It seems that, in its revised form, the Verbal-opposition Theory may go a long way toward providing a satisfactory account of metaphor — if it can be defended against two possible lines of objection that are suggested by recent developments.

The first objection might be raised by those who are committed to an extensionalist theory of meaning, as opposed to an intensionalist one. The Verbal-opposition Theory cannot be formulated without speaking of properties (that is, qualities and relations) that are incompatible with each other; but the extensionalist does not believe that there are such things as properties. Could we not, he might ask, get along without the concept of incompatibility, and treat metaphors as simply a special case of materially *false* statements? Of course there is a difference between saying that someone is bald when he isn't and saying that he is a lion when he isn't. But perhaps the difference is merely that the latter is more surprising, more obviously and certainly known to be untrue. We see how the speaker might make a mistake about baldness, but we don't see how he could confuse a man with a lion, and so it is the sheer improbability of the latter remark (in the light of common knowledge) that makes us reject it literally and take it metaphorically — rather than an internal opposition of meaning.

We could make out a case for this Improbability Theory of metaphor, and we can even support it by examples of certain degenerate cases of metaphor that may be analyzable in this way. For example, the joker says, "I was in Philadelphia once, but it was closed."[24] Is this really self-contradictory? True, the word "closed" is ordinarily, and most appropriately, applied to individual enterprises, like stores and museums, which have doors that can be locked and bolted. But perhaps without stretching the term very much, a whole city could be literally closed, too. Let us suppose so. In that case, the peculiar metaphorical effect — the denigration of the vitality of Philadelphia night life — must depend on our rejecting the statement as false out of hand, because it is so absurdly unlikely. Yet granting that this verbal maneuver occurs, it does not cover all the cases. At the opposite extreme is oxymoron. A reviewer in the *Reporter* a while back described the literary figures of the Beat Movement as "writers who don't write who write." That is not merely improbable. And it seems to me that metaphors, for the most part, have something of this built-in self-controversion, quite distinguishable from the Philadelphia crack. Borderline cases there of course must be, where there is a not-too-remote possibility of taking the modifier in a way that will literally apply to the subject: for example, the phrase "bak'd with frost," in Shakespeare's *Tempest* (I, ii, 256), where "bak'd" could mean "thickened," and so the whole expression could have been literal in Shakespeare's time.[25]

The second objection to the Verbal-opposition Theory might be put this way: even if there are properties to be opposed, they are not, in ordinary language, so fixed in the designation of general terms that sharp and clear contradiction can occur. It is conceded that "brother" and "male sibling" may be practically perfect synonyms, as far as their central meanings are concerned (ignoring their connotations), and so "female brother" is internally contradictory — though not much of a metaphor, of course. But the thesis is that for most of the interesting words, the rules are not so definite, and so when these words are used metaphorically it cannot be because we detect an incompatibility of meaning on the level of designation.

Professor Michael Scriven[26] has argued that the word "lemon" has, in fact, no defining properties in the traditional sense — that is, properties that *must* be present if the word is to be correctly applied to an object. He quotes Webster's definition, "The acid fruit of a tree (*citrus limonia*), related to the orange," and this does not seem to give necessary conditions of lemonness, since it would not be a contradiction to say that a lemon grew on a banana tree, or no tree at all. Scriven, however, goes further, and claims that there is no single property of lemons that is individually necessary, if many others are present. And he holds that the same is true of most general terms in common use. They designate what he calls "cluster concepts," and have "criteria" of application, but not necessary conditions.

This important idea, if it can be sustained, would require some reformulation in the Verbal-opposition Theory as I have stated it above. It would not destroy the theory by implying that if the theory is true then the word "lemon" cannot be used metaphorically — as it evidently can. Scriven himself speaks of literal meaning as having "a shifting boundary beyond which only misuse and metaphor lie."[27] If "lemon" has no necessary conditions, then it cannot be placed in a verbal context where some necessary condition is logically excluded, but it may be placed in a context where so many of its criteria are excluded that it cannot be literally applied — as when a second-hand car turns out to be a lemon.

I am not convinced that "lemon" and other ordinary words have *no* necessary conditions, and Mr. Scriven now holds his former view only in a modified form. I should think, for example, that having a certain organic texture —instead of being made of wood or wax — would be a necessary condition of lemonness. Surely being a material object is a necessary condition — a "spiritual lemon" would either be not literally a lemon or not literally spiritual. The questions involved here are subtle, too subtle for this occasion. For example, if I were suddenly to come upon an object otherwise exactly like a lemon, but six feet in diameter, I suppose I could be persuaded to call it a giant "lemon" — I really haven't made up my mind. Does this show that I now use the property of being small-sized only as a "criterion," but not as a defining property, of lemons? Perhaps so — yet if someone says an object is a lemon *without* adding any remarks about its unusual size, I am justified, I think, in deducing that it is small. Perhaps we could follow a suggestion of the late Arthur Pap[28] and others who have discussed the "open texture"[29] of empirical terms, and weight the criteria as more or less required: distinguishing "degrees of meaning." Then we might identify a metaphorical modifier as one placed in a context where one of its more stringently required conditions is excluded. Even if small size is not an indispensable property of lemons, it might be a fairly central one, in which case a context that opposed this property would be enough to throw the word into a metaphorical posture.

This question I leave open here, satisfied for the present if I have shown that the Verbal-opposition Theory not only explains quite well a number of acknowledged features of metaphor, but makes no assumptions that a sound philosophy of language would be unwilling to grant.

1. Reprinted from *Philosophy and Phenomenological Research* 22 (March 1962) 293-307.

2. "William Wordsworth: Notes Toward an Understanding of Poetry," *Kenyon Review*, XII (Summer 1950): pp. 498-519.

3. T. S. Eliot, *Four Quartets*, New York: Harcourt, Brace, 1953, p. 16.

4. "Poetry: I. The Formal Analysis; II. The Final Cause," *Kenyon Review*, IX (Summer 1947): 436-56, (Autumn 1947): pp. 640-58.

5. *The Prose Style of Samuel Johnson*, New Haven: Yale University Press, 1941 (Yale Studies in English, Vol. 94), p. 66.

6. Lane Cooper, trans., *The Rhetoric of Aristotle,* New York: Appleton, 1932, p. 192.

7. *The Well Wrought Urn,* New York: Reynal and Hitchcock, 1947, p. 29. The New Variorum Edition, ed. H. H. Furness, 5th ed., Philadelphia: Lippincott, 1915, pp. 160-61, shows amusingly what a nagging puzzle this metaphor has been to Shakespearean explicators.

8. In his chapter on metaphor in Paul Henle, ed., *Language, Thought, and Culture,* Ann Arbor: University of Michigan Press, 1958, ch. 7, a development, and also a modification, of the view earlier set forth briefly in his Presidential Address to the Western Division of the American Philosophical Association, "The Problem of Meaning," in *Proceedings and Addresses of the American Philosophical Association,* 1953-54, Vol. XXVIII, Yellow Springs: Antioch Press, 1954.

9. *Language, Thought, and Culture,* pp. 182-83.

10. *Ibid.,* pp. 177-79.

11. *Ibid.,* p. 181.

12. *Ibid.,* p. 180.

13. Lane Cooper, trans., *op. cit.,* p. 193.

14. Henle, *op. cit.,* p. 190.

15. I take this example, but not his explanation, from R. P. Blackmur, "Notes on Four Categories in Criticism," *Sewanee Review,* LIV (October 1946): pp. 576-89. It would be, by the way, interesting to hear a defense of the reversibility of Ezra Pound's "Your mind and you are our Sargasso sea."

16. Anthony Nemetz, in a recent article, "Metaphor: The Daedalus of Discourse," *Thought,* XXXIII (Autumn 1958): pp. 417-42, bases his argument on the formula that "a metaphor consists of two parts: 1. What is said; 2. What is meant" (419); the question is, then, what is the relation between them? But this formulation gets the inquiry off on the wrong track. A metaphor is a "saying," just as a literal expression is: we can say things either literally or metaphorically, and in either case we can only be understood to mean what we can say. In a sarcastic remark, what is suggested is opposed to what is stated, but if we do not let the word "say" cover both, we are sure to think that interpreting the remark is a process of getting *around* it to a hidden intention behind.

17. *Poetic Discourse,* Berkeley and Los Angeles: University of California Press, 1958 (University of California Publications in Philosophy, No. 33), pp. 108-110.

18. See Walker Percy, "Metaphor as Mistake," *Sewanee Review,* LXVI (Winter 1958): pp. 79-99. Percy shows interestingly how there can be "mistakes which . . . have resulted in an authentic poetic experience" (80). Yet he too seems to weaken at the end, when he speaks of "that essential element of the meaning situation, the authority and intention of the Namer" (93).

19. See *Aesthetics: Problems in the Philosophy of Criticism,* New York: Harcourt, Brace, 1958, Ch. III.

20. The part that is new (to me) in my present account of metaphor did not occur to me until after, and in the light of, the papers by Mr. Henle and Mrs. Hungerland, who were my fellow-symposiasts when the present paper, in a different form, was read before the 17th annual meeting of the American Society for Aesthetics, Cincinnati, Ohio, Oct. 29-31, 1959. Mr. Henle's criticism of the Verbal-opposition Theory as incapable of explaining the element of novelty in metaphorical meaning, and the discussion that followed the papers, led me to the present line of thought.

21. *Of Holy Living,* ch. II, sec. 3, in *Works,* ed. C. P. Eden, Vol. III, London 1847, p. 56. Mr. Henle used this example in his symposium paper.

22. These personality metaphors have been interestingly investigated by Solomon E. Asch, "On the Use of Metaphor in the Description of Persons," in H. Werner, ed., *On Expressive Language,* Worcester: Clark University Press, 1955, and "The Metaphor: A Psychological Inquiry," in R. Tagiuri and L. Petrullo, eds., *Person Perception and Interpersonal Behavior,* Stanford: Stanford University Press, 1958. See also Roger Brown, *Words and Things,* Glencoe, Ill.: Free Press, 1958, pp. 145-54.

23. This is the way I interpret Wallace Stevens' poem, "The Motive for Metaphor" (*Collected Poems,* New York: Knopf, 1955, p. 286): metaphor enables us to describe, to fix and preserve, the subtleties of experience and change ("the half colors of quarter-things" in springtime), while words in their standard dictionary designations can only cope with

The weight of primary noon,
The A B C of being,
The ruddy temper, the hammer
Of red and blue . . .

It seems to me quite correct to say that new metaphors enlarge our linguistic resources, even if they do not "expand meaning" in the narrow sense objected to by J. Srzednicki, "On Metaphor," *The Philosophical Quarterly,* X (July 1960): pp. 228-37.

24. Another example has been given by Kenneth Burke, "Semantic and Poetic Meaning," in *The Philosophy of Literary Form,* Baton Rouge: Louisiana University Press, 1941, p. 144 — "New York City is in Iowa" can mean that the influence of New York stretches out, like its railway tracks, into the West.

25. See the interesting papers by Allan Gilbert, "Shakespeare's Amazing Words," *Kenyon Review,* XI (Summer 1949): 484-88, and Andrew Schiller, "Shakespeare's Amazing Words," *Kenyon Review,* XI (Winter 1949): pp. 43-49.

26. "Definitions, Explanations, and Theories," in Herbert Feigl, Michael Scriven, and Grover Maxwell, eds., *Minnesota Studies in the Philosophy of Science,* Vol. II: *Concepts, Theories, and the Mind-Body Problem,* Minneapolis: University of Minnesota Press, 1958, pp. 105-7.

27. *Ibid.,* p. 119

28. *Semantics and Necessary Truth,* New Haven: Yale University Press, 1958, p. 327.

29. Friedrich Waismann, "Verifiability," *Proceedings of the Aristotelian Society,* Supplementary Vol. XIX, London, 1945, pp. 119-50. Cf. Georg Henrik von Wright, *A Treatise on Induction and Probability,* London: Routledge and Kegan Paul, 1951, ch. 6, sect. 2, and Pap. *op. cit.,* chs. 5, 11.

Pictorial Meaning, Picture Thinking, and Wittgenstein's Theory of Aspects

Virgil C. Aldrich

I

Wittgenstein has a theory of pictorial meaning and picture-thinking which I want to develop here, with constructive suggestions leading beyond his position but consonant with it. This mission will be accomplished by considering first the remarks about images and pictures and the logic of their language, then his theory of "aspects" with its portent for aesthetics and more generally for a philosophy of modes of perception and expression. His position comes to head in his *Philosophical Investigations,* so the following will focus on it as text.

Some expressions, Wittgenstein says, "say" nothing at all; they give us pictures. Such a picture *"seems* to determine what we have to do, what to look for, and how — but it does not do so, just because we do not know how it is to be applied. . . . . Asking whether and how a proposition can be verified is only a particular way of asking 'How d'you mean?' The answer is a contribution to the grammar of the proposition" (PI, p. 112e). Such expressions "may lead me to have all sorts of images; but their usefulness goes no further" (p. 111e). "A picture is conjured up which seems to fix the sense *unambiguously.* The actual use, compared with that suggested by the picture, seems something muddied" (*ibid.*), but examination shows that these pictorial "forms of expression are like Pontificals, which we put on perhaps, but with which we cannot do much, since we lack the effective power which would give this clothing meaning and purpose" (p. 127e).

An example is the picture or image that accompanies the use

93

of "above" and "below," in relation to "right-side up" and "upside down," when one speaks of the people below us on the other side of the earth as upside down. The *picture* is "correct," as an accurate drawing would show, or even as we would see through an adequate telescope at the right distance from the planet. But this is proof that it must not be mistaken as the meaning (the "Fido"-Fido mistake) or even as prescribing the "use" of the expression. In short, from the picture by itself we cannot tell the use and the meaning. "What is to be done with the picture, how it is to be used, is still obscure" (p. 184e), as in the case of saying that "though the ether is filled with vibrations the world is dark; but one day man opens his seeing eye and there is light" (*ibid.*). Wittgenstein says that this does "describe a picture," which of course it is quite possible to do in general for pictures; but elsewhere he gets to the subtle and main point, namely that the picture as an image is *evoked* by the expression, which in this respect "gives no information"; the expression just "calls up" the image (p. 100e). (Also "conjures up"; see above). This non-statemental use is better exemplified by saying that five o'clock here in the afternoon is the same as five o'clock "on the sun." This does not *describe* even just a picture or image; it evocatively expresses an image, teasing the user into supposing that some state of affairs (a time on the sun) is being described. This is *unlike* the numerous other cases in which, when the picture is present, "the application as it were comes about of itself" (p. 126e). Yet, it is never the picture *per se* that redeems the case for sense or meaning. Wittgenstein might have been less ambiguous about this. He seems at times to be saying that in *some* cases the meaning is prescribed or fixed by the picture. For example, we see the afternoon sun at a familiar angle to the horizon and *from the picture* of this could properly say that it is five p.m. there and then (if not on the sun). Similarly for "above" and "below" in the limited case of a visualized mountain (pictured or as perceived) where we say, with the image or percept in view, that the observation tower at the summit is above the plain below. Thus the picture or percept seems, if not to be the meaning, at least to prescribe it — the use.

But I think Wittgenstein's intention is not to say this. Even in these cases, it is not the picture or image *per se* that redeems the case for the significant use of "above" and "below" or the five p.m. statement, but rather the contextual control on the use including something more than just the picture. This is why the use, or the rule of use, changes with a sufficient modification of context. To date events on the sun involves an unusual extension of context, such that astronomical timing will be extraordinary, in the sense of introducing technically controlled terms related to unusual frames of reference. Wittgenstein's feel for the connexion of significant use with the rest of the situation (including the language which he sometimes calls a "form of life") is excellent, though his notion of this is coloured with the dynamic analogies an engineer or mechanic would naturally employ — language "idles" when disconnected from the body (the rest of the machine) of the context; the knob connected with nothing; the brake or lever that functions in connexion with other parts of the machinery; the "friction" or "skidding" of terms in use, in the "field of force" of the language (p. 219e), etc. All this makes an excellent point, which is comparable with that of functionalism or operationism, but more subtle, and less spoiled, by a too general notion of context and function, which Wittgenstein replaces by the notion of language games that may be very unlike one another. But the point is, however, that his intention is to say that the picture or image is *never, per se,* the meaning or the use, or its determinant. The arrow, pictured perceptually or as image, does not point *per se;* its sense (direction, reference) is a function of its use.

There is a temptation to identify the pictures evoked (not stated) by an expression as a part of its meaning, and to call it the "pictorial meaning," distinguishing this from what has been referred to as its "cognitive" use if any.[2] The distinction was comparable with what Wittgenstein had in mind when he complained that the image as pictorial evocatum does not "determine what we have to do, what to look for and how," though it is a sort of concomitant of the expression, the kind that pontificates its "meaning" if any. Wittgenstein's restriction on "the meaning" is in favour of what was called cognitive meaning, which had some connexion with being observationally falsifiable or verifiable at least if making "factual" cognitive sense. He too recognizes a relation of meaning to "Whether and how the proposition can be verified" (p. 112e).

This brings up the question of the criterion of truth, if any, for expressions of the pictorial or image-formulating sort, not functioning as statements based on "observation" of objects.

According to Wittgenstein, in this case, there is no significant question of justification or criterion for the speaker himself who "has" the image, and only the criterion of his say-so, together with the context of his behaviour and character, for the others who "get" what he says. I used to stress the possible "having" (not the knowing) of the image by all the participants to the communication as the condition of its pictorial significance, and the character-context of the user as the criterion of its truthfulness. I see now, however, the problem of the meaning of identity or even similarity claims, that several people have "the same image" (or sensation).[3] Wittgenstein's notion of "aspects," discussed below, sheds light on this question.

Dualistic or subjectivistic epistemologists, or simply plain people, who say of sensations that they are private "objects" knowable only by introspection on the part of those who have them, are like one who has a beetle in his box and says: "I can know what a beetle is like only by peering into *my* box" (see p. 100e). Wittgenstein's point is that such picture-thinking jeopardizes the notion of "object" (*ibid.*). The (subtle) conclusion is that such talk regarding sensations like pain is meaningless, not because a sensation *is* an object though not quite of the beetle sort, but because the language of sensations sometimes does not have the object-describing use. Its function may be exhibitive; it then manifests the sensation (p. 104e). This is one of the numerous and various functions of language. With this suggestion, we are ready to examine and elaborate Wittgenstein's conception of "aspect."

II

Wittgenstein's theory of "aspects" — and it is a *Lehre* not just a *Tatigkeit* — develops his thinking about pictures and images, and what "noticing" of them amounts to (PI, section xi), whether it is interpreting, perceiving, or imagining, etc. Since my own thinking on the matter has developed in this direction, with results different in significant detail from his, I shall dwell on some of his dicta, and then move on, in conclusion, to what I take to be the fuller statement of the point.

An aspect, according to Wittgenstein, is something that can

dawn on one, in a change of aspects, during a perception of something. One sees a drawing (Jastrow) now as a rabbit, now as a duck (p. 194e). Call this a picture-object, having aspects that do not appear simultaneously. The significant point − not stressed by Wittgenstein in this context − is that the criterion for the truthfulness of expressions reporting an aspect in a change of aspects, even though these are not just "images," is very like that for image-reports, that is, the say-so of the seer in the context of the situation. Noticing an aspect, seeing something as something, is not, strictly, a part of perception (p. 197e). Yet, in our picture-object case, neither is it simply imagining something, since there is a sense in which the aspect *can* be presented for notice to anyone who isn't generally "aspect-blind" (p. 213e). In fact, an aspect is described as that which can be made to figure "permanently in a picture" (p. 201e) − in *another* picture that captures and makes it patent.

This makes an aspect something like an image "in contact with" a percept. "It is as if an image came into contact, and for a time remained in contact, with the visual impression" (p. 207e). One can say that he "sees" the whole or the combination, though strictly the awareness of the aspect alone is not perceptual − not "a part of perception."

Yet, there are aspects which combine with what is perceived in an imaginative way. One may see a triangle, lying on its longest side, as if it had toppled over from a shorter one as initial base. This takes imagination (p. 207e), though it can still be included in what "seeing" sometimes means. If the triangle *had* toppled, this is precisely how it would look to anyone taking a good look at it. In this aspect, the triangle is imaged instead of perceived. And how it appears in this respect is reported in a statement whose truthfulness criterion presumably is like the image-or sensation-report criterion. The difference is that there is something for two or more people to "see" in the triangular object case − something perceptibly there, in contact with which the image is appearing. Or, to use Wittgenstein's better way of putting it, the thing in question is being seen as in a certain state, which seeing is partly imaginative.

Even a colour can have an aspect, more conspicuously when it is in a painting. It can be seen as voluminous and radiant, though it is *perceptibly* flat and by itself perhaps dull. Wittgenstein says: "How is it even possible for us to be tempted to think that we use a word to *mean* at one time the colour known to everyone — and at another the 'visual impression' which *I* am getting *now*? How can there be so much as a temptation here?" His answer is:

I don't turn the same kind of attention on the colour in the two cases. When I mean the colour impression that (as I should like to say) belongs to me alone I immerse myself in the colour — rather like when I "cannot get my fill of a colour." Hence it is easier to produce this experience when one is looking at a bright colour, or at an impressive colour-scheme (p. 96e).

This description does not occur in the portion in which Wittgenstein is explicitly developing his theory of aspects, but it certainly is a part of it. In that portion, he does however say that "in conversation on aesthetic matters we use the words 'You have to see it like *this,* this is how it is meant'; When you see it like *this,* you see where it goes wrong" (p. 202e).

Wittgenstein does not develop this theory of aspects beyond such suggestions. This leaves considerable juice yet to be squeezed out of the orange of the aspect-category. Let me conclude with an indication of what pictorial meaning and picture-thinking are as aesthetically matured, in the light of these previous basic or elemental considerations. Progress in this direction is a crying need. The prior task of isolating the sort of pictorial use of expressions which is a *liability* to making sense, or at cross-purposes, has been sufficiently well done. There is now the other mission to accomplish — discerning and describing the deliberate use of expressions primarily with their image-exhibiting function in view.

Unlike Wittgenstein, I propose to distinguish this as a major kind of use, involving a "purpose" different from what he takes to be the ordinary and therefore primary one relative to "what we have to do" and how the image or picture is "to be applied" (see above). I shall argue that the reason people so readily go wrong about this ordinary, work-a-day meaning, subserving the engineering intelligence, is precisely because these expressions *in common use* also have the image-exhibiting function, fusing with the other one which I call "literal," and on a par with it relative to the question of priority. Both are initially present and viable in the "plain talk" of non-special familiar conversation, each to be distinguished and separately developed under its own special controls, into a technical mode of expression – the scientific (literal) and the aesthetic.

Wittgenstein has himself made remarks that seem to justify this recognition of several large functions or purposes of language-games.

> . . . A picture of the object comes before the child's mind when it hears the word. But now, if this does happen – is it the purpose of the word? – Yes, it *can* be the purpose. I can imagine such a use of words. . . . (Uttering a word is like striking a note on the keyboard of the imagination.) But in the language [under consideration] it is not the purpose of the words to evoke images (p. 4e).

What I suggest is that, since the pictorial purpose is common and even occasionally becomes prevalent· and systematic, that there are (at least implicit) rules for *this* language-game, defining the "operating with signs" which I am calling "picture-thinking." The narrator and *a fortiori* the poet are the experts at this. Moreover, since "seeing" even as elemental involves a noticing of aspects and changes of aspects, such pictorial meaning – the image-exhibiting *use* of expressions – may be a formulation objectively grounded in, and developing, "experience" of things. Of course, this proposition makes crucial the question about the difference between such meaning relative to aspects and its rules or controls on the one hand, and, on the other, meaning in relation to things as perceived – "objects" of the routine perception which, according to Wittgenstein, must be distinguished from "noticing" of aspects and their changes. My anticipatory hunch is that this difference, even when the aspect in question is not the elementary sort Wittgenstein had in mind, is going to appear very like the difference he described, involving the two criteria (image and object) of truth. An amplification of this thought will conclude this essay.

Consider a large light tan tapestry hanging on the maroon-dark wall of a museum, one side of the rug being better illuminated than the other. In routine *observation* of these as objects, the light and dark surfaces appear all in the same flat plane. But, to one who "immerses himself in the colors" (*loc. cit.*) seeing them as colour-expanses, not as qualities of wall and rug, an aspect emerges for notice. Looking exclusively at the area in which the brilliant side of the tan expanse meets the dark expanse of maroon, the two planes of colour appear to form an angle to one another, protuding at the junction towards the point of view, like the corner of a building. The artist (who "gets his fill of the colours") sees this aspect, and it is his business to make it figure *"permanently* in a picture" (*loc. cit.*). He manipulates pigment on canvas in a way that makes one readily see the angularity and volume of the colour-expanse scheme in what is called the space of the picture, distinct from the flat plane of the canvas, or of the museum wall. Thus he augments the condition in which "it is as if an *image* comes into contact with the visual impression" (*loc. cit.*), with special attention to the image and for its sake.

But the important consideration concerns the use or meaning of the painting. The artist shows his work of art to you and either you see what it means if you already know how to "look at it this way and that" (*loc. cit.*); or he tells you, saying, "See the angle formed by these areas of colour, protruding here, receding there," and all at once you exclaim, "A house!" This expression "is related to the experience as a cry is to pain" (p. 197e). However, like the artist's remark, it is also a report. "The very expression which is also a report of what is seen, is here a cry of recognition" (198e). While you are trying to see what is alleged to be there by the artist, before you notice it, the criterion for you of the veracity and adequacy of the artist's expression, in his words and in the painting, is his say-so, in the context including his character and general competence as artist. This truly suggests that the work of art is a part of the artist's language, a non-verbal term in his use, and that it means the aspect-as-image which it makes salient or exhibits for the appropriate sort of looking. This is the work of art (the painting) *as aesthetic object.* Moreover, the work of art "means" the aspect under the same criterion as the verbal expression truthfully means the image that the artist notices, and which he subsequently presents "in contact with the visual impression," by the magic of the medium. I shall conform to the spirit of Wittgenstein's assertion that such noticing is *imagining,* not a part of *observing,* by stipulating this as the use of these terms. "Perceiving" or "seeing" will then, by my stipulation, be the inclusive term, meaning either the observational or the imaginative mode of awareness — two ways of looking. And, correspondingly, there will be the "object" in each of the two special senses, comprehending what is there either as object of observation or of imagination. Finally, there will be the "object" as "simply present" for perception *simpliciter* as the basic mode of awareness methodologically prior to the ramification into the two special modes, observational and imaginative. Language in its familiar non-technical use as "plain talk" is the idiom of "data" in this large, neutral sense. These remarks concern the various ways in which one looks at the thing — how you look at it, and how, accordingly, you express it.

The object-as-imaged, or as aspect, is *exhibited* by the medium of expression, pigment or words. I have called this the image-exhibiting function of the expression, whose meaning on this count I call pictorial. The operating with, or using, the various media this way, is called picture-thinking. In the verbal expression, where this becomes poetic, the image breaks the sort of contact it has with sense-impressions in painting and music, but is nevertheless exhibited for imaginative notice, at a sharper remove from things as observed. (But not from things as *perceived;* the featuring of the image-aspect in the poetic work of art or medium retains and clarifies the thing-as-imaged which is a basic part of the perceptum — a part made conspicuous by technical exclusion from it of the appearance of the thing-as-observed.

The rhythm of the poem may formulate not only the visual aspects but also the others, auditory, etc., if any. Moreover, in this mode of expression by rhythmic verbal presentation — an imaginative enactment of the theme — the aspect is exhibited as a sophisticated image subtle enough to satisfy the requirements of an object of aesthetic "vision" or experience. I am thinking of the way in which Stephen Spender looked at the ocean from the cliff-top on a summer afternoon, or Dante looked at Beatrice. Then the aspect, imaginatively prehended and presented in the poem, is an image which in turn *has* an aspect. In Spender's case, the aspect of the surf and the bend of the shore demarcated by the glitter of sunlight in the vast stringed-harp image in boundless blue space. But this itself presents a second-order aspect — life's finite vibrations (harp-strings) or activities merging into the stillness of infinite death. This is commonly called the "meaning" of the poem, but is, in its aesthetic relevance and function, an aspect of an aspect of the perceptum, to be imaginatively noticed. Else the "meaning" is given in the literal interpretation, and this is very different from the pictorial meaning which the picture-thinking of the artist has in view, and which his way of operating with signs tends to exhibit, for the appropriate sort of looking.

The sense of illumination, of revelation, that goes with the aesthetic experience is accounted for by the aspect-category. Just as on the basic level of perception *simpliciter* one discovers the "what" of the perception when, in a flash, he sees it as, say, a rabbit, so for the more imaginative noticing of aspects, and aspects of aspects. This is the "theoretic" sense of the aesthetic expression, as of the "language of realization"; it is not to be identified with the sense of the literal paraphrase. The pictorial or artistic use of the terms, for the sake of the aesthetic realization or vision, is not the literal use. Yet it illuminates the nature of things — it explains them, unless "explanation" is stipulated to mean what only the literal and scientific formulation achieves. (This restriction has an advantage, distinguishing the light that art sheds, as illumination, from that of literal statement which, when developed and systematic, is scientific explanation.)

The suggestion that the "literal" use is not primary but a special mode of expression under the control of a special way of looking called "observing," raises the question of where to place "ordinary" use. This is frequently thought of as identical with the literal, but only among specialists influenced by the scientific temper of our time. If ordinary use is less partially viewed, it is seen as the non-special, familiar "plain talk" which is big with the potentialities that, under special abstractive techniques or controls, become progressively articulate as scientific (literal), poetic and religious parlance, ramifying out from the neutral matrix of meaning, according as this or that special way of looking takes precedence over perception *simpliciter* and the accommodating things present in it.

A distinction should be noticed between the criterion of language in its *literal* image-exhibiting function, and in the aesthetic case. In the literal use, it is senseless to ask "Do you see what I see?" where the image is a clear-cut case of an erratic "visual sensation" or a mere fancy. But not in the aesthetic case, though an image is also involved. The way in which the artist formulates his subject matter, and the parlance of art-critics, show that the image-aspect of something is in question, and *this* can, in principle, be "seen" by anyone who is not aspect-blind. Such seeing is not "observing," but it *is* perceiving, in the imaginative mode.

1. Reprinted from *Mind* 67 (1958) 70-79.

2. I did this in my "Pictorial Meaning and Picture-Thinking," 1943, republished in Feigl and Sellars, *Readings in Philosophical Analysis,* 1949. The narrow restrictions in that essay are lifted in the present one.

3. See my "Images as Things and Things as Imaged," *Mind,* April 1955.

Art and the Human Form

Virgil C. Aldrich

[Part II]

Now, with the notion of the human form in view, as itself in some way an "expressive portrayal" of something or other, *not* just a material thing with a characteristic shape, mass, and motion, I proceed to its elucidation in the light of the notion of metaphor. This will help to bring the whole matter down to earth, while relating it to art. The treatment of this will conclude the essay, and be shorter than the preceding philosophical account, though it is crucial to the whole of what I am trying to accomplish on this occasion.

People are accustomed to thinking of metaphor in its linguistic form only. A metaphor, in this restricted sense, is a saying that A *is* B, where literally A is *like* B in some respects. Thus the metaphor is short for a verbalized comparison. This is the comparison theory of metaphor. An alternative is what I shall call the "function" theory, according to which what the metaphor expresses ("shows") is not reducible to a comparison of two or more similar things in a simile, but is a function of them. There are reasons for taking the latter theory to be preferable to the former. Usually the disputants stay on the linguistic level during the dispute, trying to browbeat one another with just the linguistic facts of the case, imagined and real. These linguistic pros and cons are not enough. For a decision about how to interpret metaphor, one must move down to what is experienced, in what situations; and then, with this in view, judge the issue of reducibility-or-not. It is not only a question of what-one-*says*-when (Austin) but what-one-*sees*-when.

Take, first, the case of your looking at the picture of a mountain, Cezanne's *Mont Sainte-Victoire,* for example. What do you see? It would be proper and natural to answer that you see a mountain. Of course, you could be looking at *and seeing* the *picture,* the painting, as you would tend to do if you were not sure what it is a picture of. Then you could be said to be seeing something that, in some meagre respects, is like a mountain. Moreover, if you were aware of what a mountain is like, and of the picture's resemblance to it, the report of your seeing the *painting* could read: you see the picture, knowing that it (schematically) resembles a mountain.

But this does *not* report what you see when, looking at the picture, you see not the painting of a mountain but a mountain, as you naturally said at first. Then what you *see* is neither the pigmentation on canvas, *its* colors and contours, its resemblance, etc., on the picture's side; nor is it the "actual" mountain that sat for Cezanne's painting years ago, the one whose height can be metrically determined — all this on the side of what is external to the picture or of what it represents, which need not actually exist at the time of seeing the mountain in picture space. What then *do* you see, if neither the picturing paint, nor what the painter looked at for model, nor their schematic resemblance? Whatever else this is, it is at least the animation of the picture. The picture comes alive with it, so much so that when you see this its soul, you are overlooking both the material of the work of art and the "material mountain" external to it as its subject-matter. However, since *some* awareness (perhaps cognitive) of both of these factors, and of the resemblance, is necessary to seeing the mountain in the medium of the picture, I suggest that what you see is a function of these in the form of an idea or image of a mountain that the painting *bodies forth,* or puts it thus on visual exhibit. So it is a *visible* metaphor, a metaphor that you *see.* And what you thus see is *not* reducible to seeing the painting and that it is like a mountain in certain meagre respects. Picasso said, "My sculptures are *plastic* metaphors; it's the same principle as in painting." One *sees* these metaphors, or he is metaphor-blind. The analysis of what is thus seen on the model of the reductive comparison theory is a mistake.

Now I get to the basic point. This time you are looking at the mountain (Mont Sainte-Victoire), not at a painted picture of it. But, even in this direct visual encounter with the thing itself, something like picturing is going on, in *some* sense. To get this sense is to understand the fundamental importance of the human form, in itself and in relation to the art of visual representation. Quite recently, an essay appeared called "The Picturing in Seeing."[2] This theme is an old one in the history of philosophical and psychological theories of perception. I give it here a new twist, in conclusion.

Again I ask you, what do you see? this time as you look across the fields at Mont Sainte-Victoire, and again you say "A mountain." I respond with, "Literally? Not elliptically or metaphorically?" If you are sophisticated and theoretically inclined, this will not perplex you, who have dealt before with the notion of a "perceptual image" that purports to represent something distinct from ("beyond") itself. And this something *else* that you are picturing-in-seeing is, of course, what one attempts to explore by *theoretical* investigation, or by thinking; by taking intellectual stock of the situation, not just by taking a closer look at it; a conceptual probing aimed at finding out what the thing is "in itself."

Still, you quite naturally say you see a mountain, when thus looking at one. Notice how, in this bedrock visual encounter case too, a sort of comparison theory suggests itself as the analysis of the experience, also reducing what is seen to two "similar" components. One might say, for example, that on the picturing side is the schematic retinal image and its registration by nerve-endings called rods and cones, etc., and that this configuration meagerly resembles the array of elements on the side of the thing pictured, the illuminated source called stimulus object in the theoretical account. Again, it is safe to say that these states of affairs at the subjective and objective poles of the situation are, scientifically speaking, necessary conditions of your seeing the mountain. But a report of *them* is not a report of what you simply see. (However, in this bedrock case, knowledge of them is not even presupposed, which makes it unlike the case of representation in art where some experience of picture and thing pictured does count.) Again, a sort of function theory turns out to be more sensitive to the fact of what is seen, and to the meaning of what the seer says when he reports seeing a mountain. It is a mistake to reduce this to talk about a copy compared with what it copies (what it is a copy of), the sort of mistake Descartes and John Locke made.

So, I stretch the notion of metaphor to apply also to what is seen in the bedrock or original case of visual perception — the case called "simply seeing the thing itself." In *such* cases, the image of the thing seen is "bodied forth" by the *thing itself,* in a primitive sense of "thing" defined by the conditions of its objectification for perception — light, good eyesight, etc. — and this is the sort of picturing involved in seeing the original, or in "original seeing." So, one appropriately speaks here of a *presentation* of the original thing, not a representation; this latter concept being reserved for cases where what bodies forth (embodies) the image of the thing is not the thing itself but, say, a work of visual art, where the notion of "seeing-as" applies. In the *original* case, the *seer,* with eyes directed at the thing in the light, *is* the occasion for the thing itself to get expressed or bodied forth in a colorful configuration, perspectively determined.

This brings us to the crux of the matter. If the seer has the human form, he will occasionally see something as something else, even at the bedrock level of original perception. He will see — as no nonhuman animal can — a cloud in the sky as a castle, a cliff as a lion's head. This is not at all to *mistake* something for something else because of a resemblance. Animals can do that, but are not capable of the sort of curious and contemplative seeing that seeing a castle in the sky is — seeing things "as" things they are known or at least thought not to be. *Thus does he make a spectacle of* ("objectify") *the natural picturing device itself which, in original perception, presents things to him,* where *he* functions as himself a part of the "natural" picture that expresses the contoured and colorful nature of things in perspective, with the things themselves functioning as the medium of the picture.

To see things this way is to bring action to a stand. Seeing something as something it is not mistaken to be, one's concern with what to *do* about it is held in abeyance. He stops just to look. The form of the seeing subject must be right for such speculative seeing. This is the human form, as we have already shown. With this goes the capacity for language and, with that, the full scope of the power to ideate things — to experience them in image or idea, even in their "actual" absence, thanks to metaphor, the device that "brings" and "bears" (presents) what is "beyond" (*meta-phor*), thus establishing a relation of com-presence (presence-with) between the portraying thing and the objectified thing, even in the actual absence of the latter. In such a presentation, the experience of the separate or "actual" identities of the picturing thing and the pictured object — the x seen as y — is abrogated in favor of the presentation, or of the experience of what is seen.

A work of the art of visual representation, to be seen as something which it is not thought to be, puts on explicit display the metaphorical device itself, whereby the thing not "actually" present is "re-presented." It is the occasion for the beholder to have his image, idea, or feeling of the thing *in the medium of the work,* instead of in relation to himself and to the thing itself, as in the case of original seeing. The work of visual art is therefore an occasion for the beholder to *see* in it the human psyche in its characteristic metaphorical depictive action, here however bodied forth for contemplation in the art work, not in this aesthetic case enlisting his own body as it does in the "natural" picturing involved in original seeing.

All this puts the notion of "psychic distance" in a new and confirming light. In the medium of a statue or painting one literally sees the human psyche at its work of metaphorical portrayal of things in perception. Thus, the art of visual representation creatively exploits its materials and media with a view to making a spectacle of the psyche at its work of presenting things in image and thought by metaphor, from the ground up.

But, you will say, all this applies to pictures or statues of anything, even of the mountain. What of the human form, "the nude, and best of all the nude erect and frontal"? (Berenson) Why should this be "the chief concern of the art of visual representation"? After all, the human psyche is one thing, the human form another, you may say in a Cartesian vein. The visual arts may indeed celebrate the psyche by putting it on exhibit in the work. *All* the arts do this. Why make so much of the human form in relation to art?

The answer is that the human psyche is itself bodied forth in the human form which, in the state of nature, is the best natural picture of the soul. The human form is, already or without benefit of art, an expressive portrayal of the psyche, the Logos, that has shaped the human form into an image, a picture, or the capacity to be conversant with, and creatively articulate about, the world; the power to make things that reveal things. Putting this whimsically, one might say that this is just what God did at first when he made the thing with the human form, animated with a vision that pictures the world. Then this being got wise to this gift of picturing-in-seeing things and became an artist, manipulating materials into works of art to make *them* come alive with *his* vision of things. To do special honor to the whole affair, he depicted the human form itself in the picture-space of the work, for he had noticed that a human being, thanks to the human form that expressively portrays him, already appears in a sort of person-space that has *some* properties of picture-space, which makes seeing a person *somewhat* like seeing a picture of something. What this cosmic something is (Logos), the artist anxiously, desperately, tries to clarify and amplify by making the human form itself the content of a work of the art of visual representation.

1. Reprinted from *Journal of Aesthetics and Art Criticism* 29 (1971) 299-302.

2. Moreland Perkins, *Journal of Philosophy* (May 28, 1970).

Metaphor and Aspect Seeing

Marcus B. Hester

Virgil Aldrich has suggested[2] the relevance of Wittgenstein's analysis of "seeing as" to aesthetic perception. He argues that aesthetic perception is identical to the peculiar type of seeing which Wittgenstein calls "noticing an aspect."[3] Wittgenstein clearly states that aspect seeing differs in kind from normal seeing. " 'Seeing as. . . .' is not part of perception. And for that reason it is like seeing and again not like."[4] We must then inquire how seeing as is like seeing and how it is unlike seeing.[5]

The essential reason why seeing an aspect differs from normal seeing is that the former type of seeing is related to having images. "The concept of an aspect is akin to the concept of an image. In other words: the concept 'I am now seeing it as. . . .' is akin to 'I am now having *this* image.' "[6] Imaginative experiences involve mental activity and thus are subject to the will, while in normal perceiving the knower is merely receptive. I can will to have certain images just as I can will to play chess. "Seeing an aspect and imagining are subject to the will. There is such an order as 'Imagine *this*,' and also: 'Now see the figure like *this*'; but not: 'Now see this leaf green.' "[7] Since seeing as is active or is in a sense willed, then it follows that ability to see as is based on "the mastery of a technique."[8] Because seeing as involves the mastery of a technique, ability to see as is an accomplishment requiring imaginative skill, the lack of which is called "aspect-blindness."[9] Such blindness is *'akin to the lack of a 'musical ear.' "[10] The first factor in aspect-blindness is that one is unable to execute this imaginative technique. This imaginative technique required in seeing as is the main distinction between it and normal seeing.

111

However, as Aldrich correctly notes, Wittgenstein does not want wholly to deny the relation between seeing aspects and normal seeing. Seeing an aspect is in some sense "like seeing. . . "[11] Seeing as is like seeing in that the aspect is in an important sense there; it is connected with an object in the public world. The aspect, though image-like, is there *in* the duck-rabbit figure in a way in which other types of imagery are not connected with public objects. Since such images are in contact with visual forms there really are cases of aspect-*blindness.* The aspect-blind person not only is unable to execute an imaginative technique but fails to see something that is there to be seen. Blindness, by definition, means that one is deprived of normal perception and fails to notice objects which are there to be seen by all normal observers. The aspect-blind person misses *something there to be seen.* Thus, though seeing as is related to the imagination, aspects are in a sense sharable. They are there to be noticed. The aspect then has a peculiar status: "It is as if an *image* came into contact, and for a time remained in contact, with the visual impression."[12] Wittgenstein then concludes that seeing as has the queer status of being "half visual experience, half thought."[13] Seeing as is like seeing in that the aspect is there in the figure, accessible to all normal observers; it is unlike seeing in that it requires mastery of an imaginative technique.

Aldrich extends Wittgenstein's analysis to aesthetic perception, which he argues is like aspect seeing. An example of aesthetic perception will demonstrate the similarity. Consider an unevenly lighted tapestry. To normal perception the tapestry appears to be flat, but to one who attempts to immerse himself in the colors,[14] as the artist does, the light and dark areas seem to meet each other at an angle. Artists attempt to embody permanently such seen aspects on their canvases; and, if they are successful, they capture the aspects in the same way that the duck-rabbit figure captures aspects of ducks and rabbits. In such a work of art it would be correct to say that the work means or intends the aspect.[15]

Aldrich also argues that imagery and aspects are essential to verbal art forms. He notes that ordinary language has both a literal descriptive function and an image-exhibiting function — the narrator and poet being skillful experts in exploiting the latter possibility. The poet is a specialist in managing this "picture-thinking."[16] Aldrich does note that the imagery excited by poetry is less bound up with a physical object, in the literal sense of "physical object." "In the verbal expression, where this becomes poetic, the image breaks the sort of contact it has with sense-impressions in painting and music, but is nevertheless exhibited for imaginative notice, at a sharper remove from things as observed."[17] Aldrich concludes his analysis by suggesting that the meaning of the poem is an aspect of the imagery.[18]

The purpose of this essay is to change and apply these suggestions of Wittgenstein, aided by Aldrich, to a specific type of art form, poetic language, and even more specifically, poetic metaphor.[19] My fundamental thesis is that poetic metaphor is a seeing as, a noticing of an aspect, between the parts of the metaphor, parts which for now I shall simply designate as the metaphorical subject and the metaphorical predicate.[20]

I

However, the statement of my thesis already shows that "seeing as" as I understand it is quite different from the "seeing as" analyzed by Wittgenstein. Certainly seeing as with regard to metaphor is very different from seeing as with regard to a visual Gestalt figure, such as Jastrow's duck-rabbit. Metaphorical seeing as is not, in its most essential mode, a seeing as related to a perceivable form. The only perceivable qualities that language has are the visual shapes of printed or written language and the sound of spoken language. The actual, visible shapes of the words on the page in the metaphorical subject are similar to the actual written words in the metaphorical predicate only in the most trivial way. The auditory form of the poem is at least more promising since poetry is an art form of language, and a most important feature of language as it is exploited by the poet is the sound of language. Perhaps then the relevant type of seeing as has to do with sound. Sound similarities are clearly exploited in many metaphors. For example, Spenser says:

And more to lulle him in his slumber soft,
A trickling streame from high rock tumbling downe,
And ever-drizling rain upon the loft,
Mixt with a murmuring winde, much like the sowne
Of swarming Bees, did cast him in a swowne.
The Faerie Queene I. xli. 136-140

In this passage the similarity between the word *sowne* in the predicate of the metaphor and the word *swowne* emphasizes to our ears the similarity which our minds tell us exists between the sleepy state of a *swowne* and the drowsy and dull sound of "swarming Bees." Sense and sound heighten each other in this sound tie, this rhyme. As Pope would put it: "the sound must seem an echo to the sense. . . ."[21] This is, however, still not the most essential type of seeing as in the metaphor. The poet clearly intends, as is shown by his grammatical red flag — the word "like" — that we are to be seeing as "between" the meaning of a "murmuring winde" and "the sowne of swarming Bees." Metaphorical seeing as has to do with the *meaning* of language, not primarily with its physical forms. Thus we must dismiss as trivial the two possible types of seeing as with regard to the *physical* poem. The visual similarity between the written words "murmuring winde" and "sowne of swarming Bees" is trivial, and the auditory similarity is not much better off.

I have thus far argued that metaphorical seeing as is between the subject and the predicate of the metaphor, and I have further indicated that I am not interpreting the phrases *the subject* and *the predicate* of the metaphor as referring only to the physical language of the poem but am claiming that metaphorical seeing as has to do with the *meaning* of language in the metaphor. Now I shall further examine the way meaning in the metaphor functions and shall claim, with Aldrich, that it is meaning functioning in its "image-exhibiting" mode.[22] Metaphorical seeing as is a seeing as between the metaphorical subject and the metaphorical predicate, either one or both of which must be image-exciting. Notice that I have not said that it is necessary for both the metaphorical subject and the metaphorical predicate to be imagistic. It is not required that both the subject and predicate of the metaphor be image-exciting. Thus the seeing as is not necessarily between two imagistic elements. Either the metaphorical subject or the metaphorical predicate may be "image poor." For example, note Shakespeare's metaphor:

Time hath, my lord, a wallet at his back
Wherein he puts alms for oblivion,
A great-sized monster of ingratitude.
Those scraps are good deeds past, which are devoured
As fast as they are made, forgot as soon
As done.
Troilus and Cressida, III. iii. 145-50.

The metaphorical subject, time, is quite abstract. All of the imagistic fullness of this metaphor is in the metaphorical predicate, the greedy beggar being compared to time. Quite often the motive for using a metaphor instead of a concrete type of description is that only through the metaphor, or perhaps most economically through the metaphor, can the abstract subject be given concreteness. Further, there are cases, though rare, in which the metaphorical predicate is abstract, or at least less concrete and imagistic than the subject of the comparison. For example, Eliot in his metaphor writes:

> Streets that follow like a tedious agrument
> Of insidious intent,
> To lead you to an overwhelming question. . . .
> "Love Song of J. Alfred Prufrock," ll. 8-10.

The predicate of the comparison, the "tedious argument," is less concrete than the subject of the comparison, the "streets."

Since metaphorical seeing as functions between the parts of the metaphor, one or both of which must be image-laden, *the metaphor* means not just the literal words on the page but the metaphor realized in its imagistic fullness while being read. *The metaphor* includes imagery. The words of the metaphor are quite literally seen or heard, and there are criteria for the meanings of these words, but the imagery is, if I may borrow Ryle's quotes, only "seen," "heard," etc. When we "see" Shakespeare's beggar this seeing is not just a species of normal seeing.[23] Hume notwithstanding, the imagery is not just a faded perception, though our imagery does have determinate qualities which are describable analogically in physical terms. In reading Shakespeare's metaphor we only "see" a greedy beggar which is compared to time.

However, this "seeing" is by no means a sort of epiphenomenal present, a sugarplum, which is an extra bonus tacked on the meaning of Shakespeare's metaphor. Metaphorical imagery is *fused with* or *involved in* metaphorical meaning. The way we find out what Shakespeare meant is by trying to "see" the "great-sized monster of ingratitude" which he describes. While trying to decipher a metaphor's meaning we picture to ourselves, and the poet helps us picture by his concrete descriptions and imagistic words.[24] As Richards would put it, we must develop "the habit of reading so as to allow the

fullest development to imagery in its sensory aspect. . . ."[25]
Metaphorical language, in being image-laden, carries with itself
a wealth of implicative fullness, a fullness of implication which
Empson claims is the distinguishing mark of poetic language.
The form of ambiguity forces the reader to open his mind to
the nest of possible implications or imagery which poetic
language has.[26] Poetic imagery is a part of poetic meaning.
True, we will "see" nothing in reading Shakespeare's metaphor
unless we *already* know the meaning of his language, implying
that the imagery is epiphenomenal. But knowing the meaning of
"time" and "great-sized monster" does not insure that one can
see time as a monster. Knowledge of the criteria of the words in
Shakespeare's metaphor is a necessary, though not a sufficient,
condition for understanding the metaphor. Nor is "seeing" the
beggar a sufficient condition for understanding the metaphor's
meaning. We are not just to "see" Shakespeare's monster but to
see it as it is related to time. It is conceivable that one know the
criteria for the words in Shakespeare's metaphor, and even
"see" the beggar described, but still be aspect-blind to the
relation between time and beggars. The metaphor's meaning
involves not just "seeing" but seeing as between the parts of the
metaphor.

Metaphorical seeing as, a seeing as involving "seeing", etc.,
leads to a realization of the relevant relationship or senses in
which time is like a greedy beggar, and a specification or
statement of this relevant relationship is a statement of the
metaphor's *meaning.* A relevant relationship is one in which the
metaphorical subject and predicate are alike in some senses, but
not in all senses. Shakespeare is trying to get us to see in what
relevant senses time is like a greedy beggar, and Eliot is
emphasizing a similarity between streets and insidious
arguments. In neither case are we to take the predicate of the
metaphor as literally asserted of the subject of the metaphor,
for to do so would be to take the metaphor as a literal
statement. The poet waves a grammatical red flag before us in
words such as "like" (Shakespeare's "like" is implicit) to
indicate that he is not making a literal statement. Shakespeare
and Eliot are trying to get us to see time as a beggar and streets
as arguments; neither is trying literally to predicate of time or
streets, beggars or arguments, respectively. The metaphorical
predicate is not, so to speak, absorbed by the subject as it is in a
literal statement. Both parts of the metaphor retain their

distinctiveness, and thus we might say that in a metaphor type-boundaries are transgressed but not obliterated.[27]

In summary, the seeing as appropriate to metaphor is a different sort from that analyzed by Wittgenstein. Seeing as with regard to the physical poem, that is, the poem taken as a visual or auditory object, is trivial. Metaphorical seeing as involves imagery associated with the meaning of language, while visual seeing as involves images related to physical objects.

II

A second clear way in which seeing as with regard to metaphor differs from visual seeing as can be seen by noticing the different problem of the respective types of seeing as. In order to introduce this further difference I shall analyze the seeing as relevant to visual Gestalts and give some symbols to the various aspects involved in this seeing as. The duck-rabbit Gestalt is a figure which is common to or has aspects of both ducks and rabbits. I argue that the relation between the duck aspect, the duck-rabbit figure, and the rabbit aspect is a transitive relationship. I shall symbolize the three by A, B, and C, respectively. If A is like B, the duck aspect like the duck-rabbit figure, and B is like C, the duck-rabbit figure like the rabbit aspect, then A is like C, the duck aspect like the rabbit aspect. The relationship of being like something is, of course, also symmetrical. Ducks and rabbits have some common Gestalt characteristics. Given these new symbols I can now more clearly show how seeing as relevant to metaphor differs from seeing as with regard to the duck-rabbit Gestalt. In Wittgenstein's example we are given B and the problem is to see A and C. In metaphor the problem is different though the act of seeing as is similar. In metaphor we are given A and C and the problem is to see B. B in the duck-rabbit figure is the common Gestalt form between ducks and rabbits. In the metaphor B is the relevant senses in which A is like C. In Shakespeare's metaphor we are given A and C, time and a beggar; and the purpose of seeing as is to discover B, the senses in which time is like a beggar, the common Gestalt, figuratively speaking, between time and beggars. Metaphorical seeing as is, figuratively speaking, a sort of visual seeing in reverse.

III

Third, and here differences with Wittgenstein's analysis are left behind, seeing as with regard to metaphor involves the same inherent duality that Wittgenstein noted of visual seeing as. He stated that visual seeing as was like seeing and again not like it. Seeing as is like normal seeing in that the aspect seen is related to a publicly accessible object; it is unlike seeing in requiring ability to execute an imaginative technique. Wittgenstein expressed this duality by saying: "It is as if an *image* came into contact, and for a time remained in contact, with the visual impression."[28] Metaphor has a similar duality. Ability to understand the metaphor's meaning does require imaginative skill. However, this imaginative technique, like the technique required in visual seeing as, has an objective basis. In this case the basis is the meaning of the language of the metaphor. The relevant sense of the metaphor, the aspect the poet is trying to get us to see between the metaphorical subject and predicate, is in an important sense *in* the metaphor, and thus it is there to be noticed by all normal readers. Just as it made sense to speak of aspect-blindness with regard to the duck-rabbit figure *because* the aspect is in an important sense there to be noticed by normal observers, so here it makes sense to speak of aspect-blindness because the aspect intended by the metaphor is there to be noticed by a normal reader. The abnormal reader, or the aspect-blind reader, would be one who knew the meanings of the words in the metaphor and could even perhaps "see" Shakespeare's beggar and still not be able to see time as a beggar. Quite often in reading a metaphor we are not aspect-blind and thus the metaphor's meaning seems to spring on us as inevitably as a perception. We immediately see the relevant relationship between the metaphorical subject and predicate. In such cases we are as convinced as when we successfully see an aspect that the meaning of the metaphor is in the metaphor and is there for all to notice. Unfortunately, critical disagreements over a metaphor's meaning too often painfully remind us that imaginative skill also is needed, and that the meaning is not there for all to notice *in the same sense* that the physical poem is there. The meaning of the metaphor is not even as accessible or there for notice in as strong a sense as the meaning of literal language is there for notice in dictionaries and common usage. Disputes over the *meaning of the metaphor* cannot be settled in the same way as disputes over the *meaning of words in the metaphor.* Still, if literary discussion of a metaphor's meaning is possible at all, it is presupposed that the meaning is accessible or there for normal readers. Wittgenstein's way of expressing this particular sense of accessibility as an image in contact with a perception is well taken, though here we will say it is imagery tied to the meaning of words in the metaphor. The aspects of the duck-rabbit figure are there for imaginative notice even though this type of seeing differs from normal seeing. The meaning of the metaphor is there for imaginative notice even though understanding in this case differs from the way we understand words in their literal senses. However, it must be noted that the imaginative seeing analyzed by Wittgenstein and the imaginative understanding I am suggesting as relevant to metaphorical meaning probably differ more from normal imaginative experiences than they do from normal seeing and understanding, respectively. Metaphorical seeing as involves imagination, but it is not the imagination functioning freely because the seeing as is tied to the meaning of the language of the metaphor, just as the image-like aspect in visual seeing as is not free, but tied to a physical form. Thus metaphorical imagery is not the free imagery of dreams but imagery controlled and restrained by poetic language.

IV

Fourth, both metaphorical seeing as and Gestalt seeing as are irreducible imaginative accomplishments. Seeing the meaning of a metaphor, as does visual aspect seeing, involves insight. Wittgenstein implies this point in noting that persons may be able to see without necessarily being able to see as. Such aspect-blindness is *"akin* to the lack of a 'musical ear.' "[29] To clarify the irreducible nature of these two imaginative techniques we need only attend to the way we would try to show someone an aspect. If we encountered a person who was aspect-blind and could not see, for example, the rabbit aspect, we might say: "Don't you see that these narrow pointed peninsulas are the rabbit's ears and this rounded curve is his nose? The rabbit's eye is here," and so on. We identify parts of the common Gestalt with the rabbit or duck aspect. If we are successful the person is apt to say: "Oh, yes. Now I see," meaning that he sees the duck or the rabbit. If we are unsuccessful, all we can do is try to cite some more common similarities between the duck-rabbit figure and the duck or rabbit aspect. There is no sure-fire way of *giving* the aspect-blind person the necessary insight, even though we may help him to see the figure for himself.

We treat cases of metaphorical aspect-blindness quite similarly. To see this similarity, attend to this metaphor by Emily Dickinson, a metaphor which is particularly appropriate because of the great number of critics who profess some aspect-blindness as to its meaning.

> After great pain a formal feeling comes —
> The nerves sit ceremonious like tombs. . . .
> "After Great Pain a Formal Feeling Comes," II. 1-2.

In a case of aspect-blindness with regard to this metaphor we might say: "Don't you see that a great pain, a great tragedy, stuns one into a stupor? One goes about one's daily tasks in a formal, unfeeling way. The nerves sit like tombs. Instead of the warmth of life which they formerly felt, now all is precise, numb, ceremonious, and cold like stones in a cemetery." We try to help someone see as with regard to the metaphor by citing relevant senses in which the metaphorical predicate is seen as the subject of the metaphor. If we sense that the aspect-blindness is due to ignorance of the criteria of the words in the metaphor, we might well show the person some stones in a cemetery or refer him to a dictionary which defines stones and nerves. The poet presupposes that his readers know the language he speaks. Often this presupposition is ill-founded, in which case the literary critic explains to the reader the background presupposed; he clarifies the criteria of the words in the metaphor. However, knowledge of the criteria, though a necessary, is not a sufficient condition for understanding the meaning of the metaphor, just as literally perceiving the duck-rabbit figure is not a sufficient condition for seeing the rabbit aspect. One might well know the criteria for the word "nerves" and the criteria for "tombs" and still not be able to see nerves sitting as tombs. An understanding of the metaphor, a grasp of the relevant senses in which nerves sit like tombs requires an openness to the text, a sensitivity to the imagery involved in the metaphor. Thus all we can hope to do is remove some of the blocks causing the aspect-blindness and thus elicit the response: "Oh, yes. Now I see." If we are not successful, all we can do is try some more loose and informal reasoning, cite more ways in which nerves sit like tombs, or draw attention to criteria of the words in the metaphor. Arnold Isenberg argues that it is not the function of critical language in the arts (this hypothetical conversation being precisely such a critical discussion) to "*afford* the experience which it purports to describe. . . ."[30] Rather, "it is a function of criticism to bring about communication at the level of the senses; that is, to induce a sameness of vision, of experienced content."[31] In my hypothetical example in which one is attempting to help a person aspect-blind to Dickinson's metaphor see its point, the relevant ways in which nerves sit like tombs are cited *in order to* get the reader to see nerves sitting as tombs. Since seeing as is an irreducible accomplishment, talk about the metaphor, analysis of its relevant senses, or emphasis on the criteria of words in the metaphor cannot guarantee that the aspect-blind person will now be able to see the metaphorical predicate as the subject, but it is the purpose of such talk to "induce sameness of ·vision, of experienced content." Bouwsma puts the same point slightly differently by saying that in poetry the meaning is in the language in a special sense. It cannot be gotten out, strictly speaking, in translations or restatements. We can only suggest that the poem be reread.[32] We cannot cause one to have the insight necessary to see nerves sit like tombs just as we cannot cause an aspect to be seen, though we can help in both cases. In both cases of aspect-blindness we call up analogies and point the person back to the original. In both cases seeing as is an irreducible accomplishment in which the imagination aids perception or reading. It is categorically impossible to reduce seeing as to a set of rules or criteria.

In conclusion, my claim is that discovering the meaning of a metaphor depends on seeing the relevant aspect between the metaphorical subject and metaphorical predicate, one or both of which must be image-laden. This type of seeing as differs from visual seeing as in that the aspect seen is associated with the meaning of language, meaning functioning in its image-exhibiting mode, instead of an aspect in contact with a visual form. Further, metaphorical seeing as has a different problem than that of visual aspect seeing. It is, figuratively speaking, visual seeing as in reverse. The metaphor states the aspects and the problem is to see the common form while in visual seeing as the common element is given and the problem is to see the aspects. Third, metaphorical aspect seeing and visual aspect seeing are similar in that both have an inherent duality. In both cases an imaginative technique is required while at the same time the respective aspects are in an important sense there to be noticed. Finally, metaphorical seeing as and visual seeing as are irreducible imaginative accomplishments. One either sees the aspect or does not see it, and there is no procedure which inevitably removes aspect-blindness. Pointing back to the original and emphasizing various parts of it are the best remedial helps.

1. Reprinted from *Journal of Aesthetics and Art Criticism* 25 (1966) 205-212.

2. Virgil C. Aldrich, "Pictorial Meaning, Picture-Thinking, and Wittgenstein's Theory of Aspects," *Mind,* LXII (January, 1958), 70-79.

3. PI (*Philosophical Investigations*), p. 193e.

4. PI, p. 197e.

5. I shall throughout this essay omit the quotes around "seeing as" because I shall be referring to the act of seeing as. Wittgenstein himself is clearly at places talking of seeing as instead of the concept of "seeing as." He no doubt would have claimed he was analyzing only the concept of "seeing as," but I doubt that such an analysis can be carried out without also talking of the intentional correlate of such a concept, namely the imaginative act of seeing as.

6. PI, p. 213e.

7. PI, p. 213e.

8. PI, p. 208e.

9. PI, p. 213e.

10. PI, p. 214e.

11. PI, p. 197e.

12. PI, p. 207e.

13. PI, p. 197c.

14. PI, p. 96e.

15. Aldrich, p. 77.

16. *Ibid.*

17. *Ibid.*

18. *Ibid.*

19. Even though my analysis is limited to poetic metaphor I think it can be extended, given certain modifications, to other types of metaphor, for example, models in science.

20. I shall also use the phrase "metaphorical seeing as" instead of the awkward circumlocution "the seeing as that is relevant to metaphorical meaning."

21. Alexander Pope, "An Essay on Criticism," 1. 365.

22. Aldrich, p. 75.

23. Gilbert Ryle, *The Concept of Mind* (London,1960), p. 250.

24. I have spoken of "deciphering" and "finding" the metaphor's meaning because a metaphor does not carry its meaning on its sleeve. There are no dictionaries telling metaphorical meaning. There are dictionaries telling the meaning of *dead* metaphors such as "the *neck* of a bottle," etc. A poetic metaphor, however, must be fresh and suggestive, and this very suggestiveness breaks out of assigned meanings. Further, there are dictionaries defining the words in the metaphor, dictionaries telling what is meant by "time" and "monster" and "streets" and "arguments" but none defining time seen as a beggar and streets seen as arguments.

25. I. A. Richards, *Principles of Literary Criticism* (A Harvest Book), p. 123; first published in 1925.

26. William Empson, *Seven Types of Ambiguity* (London, 1956), p. 91.

27. Douglas Charles Berggren, "An Analysis of Metaphorical Meaning and Truth" (Unpublished Doctor of Philosophy dissertation, Dept. of Philosophy, Yale University, 1959), p. 383.

28. PI, p. 207e.

29. PI, p. 214e.

30. William Elton, ed., *Aesthetics and Language* (Oxford, 1959), p. 142.

31. Elton, pp. 137-38.

32. *Ibid.,* p. 95.

Anxiety: Reification of a Metaphor

Theodore R. Sarbin

I

The title of this panel, Anxiety Revisited, suggests the figure of paying a call to a place which at an earlier time in one's life was especially significant and characterized by poignant memories. In real life, such visitations invariably result in disillusionment and frequently in one's questioning the basis of his beliefs about the place. Not uncommonly, looking over the old haunts leads one to the painful conclusion that he has been preserving the remains of an imaginary companion created to solve some of the problems of childhood. Whether this figure of speech has any merit remains to be seen.

Somewhat in the manner of an archeologist, I have visited "anxiety," dug around the footings, and set down my observations. Two main theses stem from these observations: The first thesis questions the utility, for our times and purposes, of the general conception of internal, psychic, or mental states of which anxiety is an exemplar; the second thesis attempts to account for the conduct of persons confronted with identifiable problems and for whom the label of anxiety is loosely used. Explicitly rejecting any dependence upon "states of mind" or similar constructs, I employ the metaphor, *cognitive strain*. It may be applied systematically to a wider variety of problems without carrying the excess baggage of the anxiety concept. I hope to show that this argument is more than a substitution of labels and that the implications for theory and practice are abundant.

125

That there is no unequivocal definition of anxiety can be readily demonstrated. A perusal of textbooks, journal articles, dictionaries, and other sources gives a confused picture. Some of the definitions are expressed in terms of overt behavior, such as tremor, stuttering, and coughing; some in terms of complex conduct such as avoidance, defense, and denial; some in terms of antecedent events such as aversive stimuli and memories of traumatic events; some in terms of physiological responses, such as heart rate, GSR, and respiratory rate; and some in terms that have no existent referents, such as apprehensions, dispositions, emotional states, states of mind, psychic states, affects, and feelings. The methods of assessing anxiety are similarly multiform. Cattell and Scheier (1961) isolated some 120 different procedures for estimating anxiety. There are probably more than this number running the course from self-report and projective tests through objective questionnaires to myographic recordings, autonomic measures, and biochemical assays.

All classifications are to some extent Procrustean, and my attempt to classify these multiple referents for anxiety must deform some of the definitions. However, the following threefold classification appears to contain all the instances.

I. Definitions that focus on avoidance behavior, ie, the responses of an organism to aversive stimuli in situations where opportunities for withdrawal are absent. The aversive stimuli may be present or may be represented by signs or symbols.

II. Definitions that focus on measures of physiological arousal or on the physiological or motoric consequents of such arousal.

III. Definitions that focus on anxiety as a psychic state or state of mind concurrently inferred from reported discomfort or distress, or predictable from a knowledge of stimulus events, or postdicted from conduct presumably activated by such a mental state. A good example of this class of definitions is May's (1950): "Anxiety is the *apprehension* cued off by a threat to some [personally significant] value. . ." (italics added).

The first and second shall not concern us in the present analysis. The behavior that follows aversive stimuli can be described satisfactorily without positing anxiety as an intervening variable. The physiological formulation has not been particularly fruitful. Physiological arousal can be produced in many ways other than by excitants that carry supposedly anxiety potentials. Further, the correlations between different indicants of arousal are generally low and unstable as are the correlations between physiological measures and other measures such as self-report, questionnaires, etc. My emphasis in this paper is placed on the third set of definitions, those that posit anxiety as a mental state intervening between stimulus events and overt or covert behavior.

Parenthetically, it is frequently the case that anxiety in the third sense is based upon the model of fear as a psychic state. The cliche is often repeated that fear is a psychic state produced by a set of objective events that signify danger; anxiety is a similar psychic state, but the precipitating events are absent or "unconscious." It is interesting to note that the original use of the word fear carried no denotation of mental states — rather the term was used to denote distal events that were dangerous, hazardous, perilous, and so on. The conversion of such denotations to mental states was one of the latter-day outcomes of those theories that required mind and mental states.

The implication of my analysis is that we discontinue the use of the anxiety construct for scientific purposes. This implication follows, to be sure, from the multifarious and confusing existent referents for the term, but mainly from the postulation that it is a psychic or mental state and that such states are somehow not in the same scientific domain as performances, responses, actions, movement, transactions, and behaviors. The mental-state doctrine holds that such activities as walking, running, lifting, pushing, laughing, and crying are events that can be described in *occurrence* terms — as doings of the body; and that such events as thinking, imagining, willing, feeling, intending, and perceiving are not describable in occurrence terms. Rather these sundry activities are carried on by an entity that is variously called mind, psyche, spirit, Geist, etc. When Descartes, in the 17th century, formulated his thesis about man and nature, he obscured his explanation by using a metaphor without regarding it as such. In the intellectual climate of the time, the soul was a fact of life. To account for his observations of self and others, he made use of the religious idiom. Since the complex behavior of knowing, thinking, doubting, feeling, etc, were not amenable to explanation through the idiom of 17th century mechanics and geometry, the only other available model was the then well-entrenched religious model of the invisible, immaterial soul. Although, as one writer points out, Descartes wrote as if the soul were a metaphor to account for otherwise unaccountable happenings, his actual behavior led to the likely inference that he regarded his soulful explanation as literal truth (Turbayne, 1962). In any case, the metaphor of one generation becomes the myth of the next, and Descartes' Ghost in the Machine continues to haunt us (Ryle, 1949) — thus, the ready acceptance of mental states as "real" entities and, as a result, the employment of mental states as intervening processes in modern psychology and psychiatry. Mental states, including anxiety, are not without functional significance. Like superstitions and delusions, they fill a gap by providing answers to difficult questions. For example, for those theorists espousing a "drive-reduction" conception of motivation, the anxiety notion does fill the gap. When learning of instrumental acts occurs in the absence of "classical" drives, eg, hunger and thirst, the positing of anxiety as a drive keeps the theory whole.

The myth of mental states, like all myths, resists extinction. In part, this resistance can be explained by the structuring processes of language. Our language contains many mental state terms that have no existent referents, only vague verbal ones. We learn these terms before we can be analytical about their origins and about the unreliability of the sensory inputs that call out these symbols. Behaviorist psychologists, positivists, and empiricists of various persuasions have tried to show that the concept of mind was a mistake based upon the transformation of a metaphor to a myth. And, as we all know from the history of science, a myth has the force of literal truth until it is exploded and replaced by a currently more useful metaphor.[2]

For our purposes we can begin our linguistic analysis of anxiety with the language of the Middle Ages. As an introduction, the natural history of word formation seems to be, first, the creation of words to denote objects and events in the distal environment, such as rain, sun, fire, clouds, rivers, people, and so on. These objects and events are mediated primarily by the distance receptors of vision and audition. Later, terms are invented for denoting proximal events, such as aches, itches, engorgements, tickles, hurts, etc. Symbols already in existence to denote distal events are borrowed through metaphor to denote proximal events. Just as distal events are mediated by auditory and visual receptors, proximal occurrences, and *not* hypothetical mental states, are mediated by somesthetic receptors. To be sure, the creation of a language to denote distal and proximal events is no mean achievement. Such languages arose to serve the purposes of men to communicate about things of importance to their survival. The achievement of a language to denote mental states, however, required a kind of *tour de force,* a special set of circumstances, because empirical events as referents for mental states could not be reliably determined.

The thesis that I want to advance is that the language of conduct was essentially a distal-proximal language before the great religious and scientific transformations of the Renaissance. This is not to say that words were absent for denoting imaginary things such as dragons and angels, but that these fictive objects were located in the distal ecology, not in a shadowy inner world. A prime example of this thesis is in an analysis of Chaucer's Canterbury Tales.[3] There is almost no direct description of the presumed internal states of the characters. The motivation to go on pilgrimages, for example, is in the world of nature and in the changing seasons. It is not described in mental-state terms. It was not until the development and widespread acceptance of religious beliefs about the existence of a separate inner life, a private, shadowy stage, that terms had to be borrowed or created to denote happenings in the ghostly world.

Not only in literature but in the prevailing scientific descriptions of this era do we find support for the notion that the referents for words were located in the distal ecology and that mental-state words were absent. The theory of humors, for example, accounted for disease and disorder. Humors were believed to be real, in the sense that blood, phlegm, and yellow bile were real. Thus, temperament was seen as the predominance of one of the humors, not as the action of mental entities. Another scientific belief of the time that illustrates the use of distal language was the notion of "natural contraries." To a fowl, the fox is a natural contrary. The avoidance behavior of a rooster upon first seeing a fox was not regarded as dependent upon a mental state of fear, but as a propensity built into the nature of beasts. The theory of demonic possession of lunatics and imbeciles was essentially a theory based upon distal rather than mentalistic concepts. The deviant behavior was seen as a result of the actions of demons that entered the body. The scientifically approved treatment was to coax or drive the demons out.

From this brief overture, let us now trace the etymology of the word *anxiety*. We discover that it came into modern English from the Middle English *anguish*. The term came into the lexicon when the effects of the great religious revivals in Europe were carried to the common man in the towns and villages. Unlike the older ecclesiastical words that denoted the more formal aspects of ritual and ceremony, the new words were intended to represent the inward and personal aspect of faith. Devotion, duty, pity, comfort, conscience, purity, and salvation were other words introduced during the 13th century coincidentally with the building of the great churches and monastic houses of medieval England (Smith, 1912).

These ecclesiastical words are unlike terms standing for distal and proximal occurrences. They are intended to denote the activities of a shadow-like spirit in a private world. However, words do not spring from the blue — they spring from metaphor. And on the theory presented here, the word anguish should have denoted events in the distal or proximal ecology *before* it was borrowed to denote a religious (and later, a mentalistic) experience. As used in medieval times, the antecedent of anxiety, *anguish,* carried the meaning of mental or spiritual suffering. But anguish was the anglicized version of the Old French *anguisse* which denoted a painful, choking sensation in the throat. Thus, we find a bodily, proximal referent for a term which had been borrowed to denote a state of mind. Since one of the commonest forms of metaphor is achieved through composing an analogy, we might reconstruct the origins of anguish as follows: A choking sensation in the throat, produced, let us say, by swallowing a chicken bone, is denoted by the term anguisse or anguish. The death of a loved one, a misfortune, recognition of sin, and similar events often lead to a similar proximal event — a globus in the throat. Here are two proximal events that share one property, namely, the discomfort or pain in the throat. To complete the analogy, their symbols are also shared; the term denoting one is employed to denote the other — ignoring the weighty fact that their antecedents are in different modalities, different idioms.[4]

It remains to demonstrate, however, that anguish became a term denoting a mental state rather than proximal events in the throat following certain social and personal happenings. The context in which mental state is used is best expressed by the polarity *inside-outside*. For an approach to the understanding of how the mental or psychical world was allocated to the inside, we suggest the following: We can identify two classes of proximal inputs. The first occurs in a context of distal events. Thus, pain in a skinned knee occurs in the context of falling on a hard, abrasive substance; discomfort in the region of the metatarsal arch occurs with prolonged walking or standing on high heels; a burning pain in the thumb occurs after clumsily hitting it with a hammer while hanging pictures, etc. The second class of proximal inputs occurs in the *absence* of recognizable distal events, such as toothache, headache, precordial pain, neuritis, gastritis, etc. Since the antecedents of the latter proximal inputs could not be located on the outside by Medieval Man, the locus of the bodily perception was taken as the causal locus, ie, inside the body. But Medieval Man had little knowledge about nor interest in anatomy. He knew in a dim way that there were some organs, tubes, fluids, and bones, and he knew there were empty spaces. So, under the authority of the preachers (and later the philosophers) he learned that an invisible, immaterial spirit resided in these otherwise empty spaces. On this kind of belief system, events for which there were no observed distal contexts could be attributed to the workings of this inside entity. So proximal events, such as lumps in the throat, which could not be related to happenings in the distal environment, to the humors, or to local, specialized demons, were related to the mental or spiritual happenings inside the person. The modern conception of anxiety as a mental and emotional state is a direct descendant in this lineage.

You will be interested to learn, as I was to discover when I prepared this paper that the word anxiety was hardly used in standard medical and psychological textbooks until the late 1930's. It was a result of Freud's writings about Angst, translated as anxiety, that the term now has wide currency. Freud's theories made extensive use of mentalistic metaphors, and his more influential theory of anxiety, published in 1923, was no exception.[5]

Before moving into the final section of my paper, I want to subscribe to the notion that there is no ultimate truth; and to the corollary that there are different ways of interpreting events. The latter corollary may be restated as the employment of different metaphors to denote events to ourselves and to others. To me, the test of whether one metaphor is better than another is the pragmatic one. Modern scientists and practitioners must ask: Which metaphor leads to implications that are useful, which helps one to achieve his purposes? That the Ghost in the Machine metaphor was useful can be established through the historical fact that it replaced the now unacceptable metaphor of demons as initiators of action. The metaphor of mental illness, which (as Szasz [1961] has argued) evolved into a myth, was for a time useful because it set the stage for 19th century humanitarians to introduce changes in the prevailing beliefs about the treatment, care, and custody of disordered persons.

To recapitulate: I have attempted to show that anxiety has many meanings, a condition that interferes with lucid communication. I have further tried to argue that anxiety as a mental state follows from certain historical mistakes occasioned by literal interpretations of metaphors. The implications of my arguments are these: the mentalistic and multi-referenced term anxiety has outlived its usefulness. Unless a convention is called to decide on more precise existent referents for the term, it would be better to discontinue employing it in scientific discourse.

II

As a replacement for the mentalistic anxiety metaphor, I propose the metaphor of cognitive strain. It is drawn, on the one hand, from a derivative of evolutionary theory, and on the other, from a working hypothesis that the world about us is knowable if we work at it. Cognitive strain may be defined without reference to excessive visceral activity, although it is doubtful whether cognitive activities such as thinking, problem-solving, and imagining can be performed without some subdued or overt motoric activities with their associated autonomic feedbacks.

The first assumption in the model is almost pure Darwinism. In order to survive, living creatures must locate themselves correctly in the world of occurrences — in the distal ecology. If a creature is inaccurate in locating himself, he is likely to become a prey to predators or to wander away from the sources of food and drink and from protective cover. Human beings also must place themselves in the ecology. But, as a result of living in social groups with norms and expectations, and with beliefs about transcendental objects, they must locate themselves in multiple ecologies. If the world of occurrences provides unclear or insufficient cues to solve the problem of ecological placement, then we have the condition of cognitive strain. The referent for the strain metaphor is a large increase in cognitive behavior. This increase occurs in two ways: (*a*) in attempts to fit what-is-now-happening (inputs) into the summaries of what-has-happened-before (the cognitive organization, the major premises); and (*b*) in attempts validly to use the multiplicity of major premises that are activated by the sensory inputs. We assume that there are optimal degrees of cognitive strain for efficient cognitive behavior just as there are optimal degrees of muscle tonus for different kinds of motoric activities.

In the present model, we can structure the world of occurrences for any person as we did in our earlier analysis into proximal and distal ecologies. The proximal ecology is the constantly varying set of stimulus inputs mediated by the somesthetic receptors, the pressures, engorgements, sensations of hot and cold, itches, pains, aches, hurts, and so on, that help to define the form and volume of the body. Under certain conditions of cognitive strain, when the autonomic nervous system is engaged, the proximal ecology may include additional inputs from visceral organs as well as from the skeletal musculature.

The distal ecology may be differentiated into five systems. They may be identified as:

The self-maintenance ecology
The spatial ecology
The social ecology
The normative ecology
The transcendental ecology.

The self-maintenance ecology includes those objects and events which a person must take into account in order to maintain the self. In a state of nature, self-maintenance would be equivalent to survival. In human cultures, self-maintenance includes such aspects of honor, face-saving, role-constancy, integrity, dignity, etc. To be alert to multifarious stimulus events, an organism maintains an attitude of vigilance, a readiness to classify an object or event as threatening, dangerous, friendly, neutral, etc. It has been suggested that the human or other animals in the vigilant posture, upon noticing a stimulus event, might be described as asking the question *What?* or *What next?* or *What is it in relation to me?* The answer that the person gives to the *what* question in the simplest case is *threat* or *nonthreat,* but the refinements of extended experience, perceptual learning, and linguistic development allow all kinds of modulated answers to be given. When the question is answered verbally, it is in the form of a *qualitative* assessment of the ecological object, signified by adjectives such as hostile, accepting, friendly, unfriendly, helpful, deterring, and so on. The complexities of dimensional attributes in the distal world must be paralleled by complexities in cognitive dimensions to make possible modulated, rather than polar, responses to the *what* question.

The inability to classify the inputs from the distal world of occurrences on dimensions of the self-maintenance ecology produces cognitive strain. Conditions leading to such a resultant include uncertainty, unpredictability, the interruption of expected ecological events, and nonoptimal stimulus inputs (overloading of the perceptual apparatus or insufficiently differentiated inputs). The instantiation of an event as threatening does not lead to cognitive strain *unless* the person has no immediately accessible adaptive techniques for dealing with the object of threat, such as, withdrawal, flight, or protective covering. In such cases, *increased vigilance follows* and other *What* and *What next* questions are asked. More acquired major premises are activated with the resultant necessity to decide which conclusions are the correct ones. Under such conditions, organismic involvement may increase. Such involvement is mediated through skeletal and visceral activity and may provide additional inputs which must also be instantiated. The necessity to instantiate multiple inputs, the increase in activated premises, and the interference from proximal inputs may increase the complexity of the cognitive organization. Thus, we may define cognitive strain as large increases in cognitive activity. In another idiom, we might say it is the search for answers to impelling questions.

The same analysis may be applied to the other ecologies, *mutatis mutandis.* In keeping with the metaphor of asking questions, we can pretend that people have readily accessible the question *Where am I?* in order to locate themselves on spatial dimensions. That such questions have a high access ordering is undeniable when a person is in a strange place, or is presented with contradictory spatial cues. The experiments of Witkin et al (1954) in which contradictory postural and visual cues to a perception of the vertical were employed show clearly what happens when the *Where am I* question cannot be satisfactorily answered. Some subjects in these experiments reported discomfort, disorientation, feelings of uncertainty, and loss of bearing in the laboratory.[6]

To locate oneself in the social ecology, one has available the question *Who is he* and the reciprocal *Who am I?* or in alternate terms, *What role must I enact?* In rigid caste and class systems, such questions are asked only infrequently, if at all. In open social systems, for example, where mobility in one social dimension is not necessarily associated with mobility on correlated dimensions, such as socioeconomic level and educational achievement, the question *Who am I* may produce cognitive strain because multiple answers may be contradictory. A recent report suggests a strong relationship between contradictory answers to questions of placement in the social ecology and the incidence of psychosomatic complaints. Jackson (1962) reports a survey study in which the respondents were classified along three social dimensions: education, occupation, and racial-ethnic background. When compared with respondents whose answers indicated consistency among the dimensions, persons whose answers indicated lack of congruence (eg, high on one dimension, low on the others) were more likely to report the presence of psychophysiological symptoms, such as dizziness, excessive perspiration, loss of appetite, trembling, dyspnea, etc. I would offer the following interpretation: Placement in the social structure is a continuing affair. The continuing need properly to locate oneself in the social ecology in the presence of multiple and contradictory cues produces cognitive strain. High degrees of cognitive strain can involve the entire organism, thus engaging the skeletal and visceral systems and providing proximal inputs to serve as referents for psychophysiological complaints.[7]

To locate oneself in the normative ecology, one must ask the question *How well am I doing?* This question always is asked in respect to some norm, value, standard, expectation, prescription, etc. In all cultures, propriety norms serve as the basis for the evaluation of many sorts of conduct. Guilt and shame are names given to the recognition of performances that do not measure up to certain kinds of norms. In achievement-oriented cultures, the *how well* question may refer to performances gauged against real or imagined standards of competence. When the answer to the *how well* question is difficult to achieve through ambiguities or contradictions in the major premises that comprise norms, then a condition of cognitive strain exists.

The transcendental ecology is an extension of the self-maintenance ecology. For human beings, there exist not only objects of a material sort but also objects that inhabit a shadowy, ephemeral, super-empirical world. Hallowell (1956) has found it useful in accounting for the conduct of various primitive groups to distinguish between the "behavioral environment and the geographical. The behavioral world includes such entities as ghosts, spirits, windigos, numina, leprechauns, angels, demons, and fairies. Persons who participate in cultures where beliefs are held about such entities engage in behavior that may be described as attempts to answer the question: *What am I in relation to these objects?* Placement of oneself in the transcendental ecology, then, calls for cognitive behavior in which occurrences serve as inputs to instantiate the behavior of these transcendental objects. Religious crises, and autistic conduct in which communication with the deity is involved (sometimes denoted by the term schizophrenic) are events that illustrate this phenomenon. Thus, failure properly to place oneself in the transcendental ecology is another origin of cognitive strain.[8]

III

Because of time limitations, I have been brief and have tried only to sketch in broad bold strokes the antecedents to cognitive strain. A few comments are appropriate regarding the implications of this model for theory-building and for clinical practice. For the former, a great deal may be said, but it can be summarized under the general heading of economy and efficiency of thought. Occam's razor — the admonition not to multiply entities needlessly — might be cited here when we argue against continuing to use mentalistic metaphors.[9]

The wise employment of the cognitive strain metaphor will point the way to a search for facts that has been absent in the use of the anxiety metaphor. At least in the present formulation, a scientist will direct his attention to antecedents of human problems, to knowable ecological events and to conduct designed to place these events in a cognitive framework. He will not be sidetracked by searching for the dynamics of a mentalistic entity. In the experimental field, related approaches have already been successfully tested. Among these, the metaphor of cognitive dissonance has been fruitfully employed by Festinger (1957).

The implications for psychotherapeutic practice are especially clear. Instead of focusing on anxiety as a mentalistic or as a physiological signaler of internal psychic struggles, the therapist will focus on the difficulties presented by a patient in coming to terms with his world. He will be particularly cognizant that the use of "anxiety-reducing" drugs, for example, is directed at the organismic *effects* of cognitive strain. He will be constrained to ask and answer such questions as the following: under what conditions is it wise — through medication or somatic treatment — to reduce inputs from the proximal ecology? Is the reduction of the patient's attention to proximal inputs a valid criterion of success in therapy?

In proposing the metaphor of cognitive strain, I am painfully aware that it does not produce the dynamic overtones now associated with the anxiety metaphor. Perhaps this is as it should be. For nearly a half century, a romantic mystique has evolved around the professional enterprise stimulated by Freud's colorful metaphors. Experienced clinicians recognize that the mystique is not justified, — and that when therapy is successful, it is not due to the purging of anxiety. Rather, it is because the patient has learned how to minimize, with his finite cognitive capacities, the strains produced in his efforts to find himself in a complex, changing, and often contradictory world.

REFERENCES

1. Cattell, R. B., and Scheir, I.V.: The Meaning and Measurement of Neuroticism and Anxiety, New York: Ronald Press, 1961.
2. Festinger, L.: A Theory of Cognitive Dissonance, Palo Alto, Calif: Stanford, 1959.

138

3. Hallowell, A. J.: Aggression in Salteaux Society, in C. Kluckhohn; H. A. Murray; and D. M. Schneider: Personality in Nature, Society and Culture, ed 2, New York: Knopf, 1956, pp 260-275.

4. Jackson, E. F.: Status Consistency and Symptoms of Stress, Amer Soc Rev 27:469-480, 1962.

5. May, R.: The Meaning of Anxiety, New York: Ronald Press, 1950.

6. Ryle, G.: The Concept of Mind, London: Hutchinsons University Library, 1949.

7. Sarbin, T. R.: A New Model of the Behavior Disorders, Nederl T Psychol 10:315-341, 1962.

8. Sarbin, T. R.; Taft, R.; and Bailey, D. E.: Clinical Inference and Cognitive Theory, New York: Holt, Rinehart and Winston, 1960.

9. Smith, L. P.: The English Language, London: Oxford University Press, 1912.

10. Snell, B.: The Discovery of the Mind, New York: Harper Torchbooks, 1960.

11. Szasz, T.: The Myth of Mental Illness, New York: W. W. Norton & Company, Inc., 1961.

12. Turbayne, C. M.: The Myth of Metaphor, New Haven, Conn: Yale University Press, 1962.

13. Witkin, H. A., et al: Personality Through Perception, New York: Harper & Brothers, 1954.

FOOTNOTES

1. Reprinted from *Archives of General Psychiatry* 10 (1964) 630-638.

2. The notion of mental states did not originate with Descartes. Snell (1960) presents an argument that the Hellenic Greeks "discovered" the mind. It is plausible to argue that "mind" is a category in Snell's cognitive structure. What the Greeks discovered, in my view, was that it was possible to talk about referents for the term *I* (ego) as it was to talk about referents for terms denoting objects in the distal world. The mind, on this construction, would be an invention. The concept of mind was probably lost in early medieval times and was discovered or recovered in the Renaissance when men became interested in talking about themselves as individuals in relation to natural and supernatural objects and also in talking about their language.

3. "Whan that Aprill with his shoures soote
   The droghte of March hath perced to the roote
   And bathed every veyne in swich licour
   Of which vertu engenered is the flour,

When Zephirus eek with his sweete breeth
Inspired hath in every holt and heeth
The tendre croppes, and the yonge sonne
Hath in the Ram his half cours y-ronne,
And smale foweles maken melodye
That slepen al the nyght with open eye,
So priketh hem Nature in hir corages,
That longen folk to goon on pilgrymages,"

Chaucer: *Canterbury Tales*

4. It is tempting to speculate on another behavioral antecedent for constructing the analogy. In the sacrament of communion, the communicant is expected to swallow, without chewing, the wafer that symbolizes the body of Christ. Acceptance of the sacrament is forbidden if one is not in a state of grace through confession. If a person were to accept the wafer at the same time recognizing that he was not in a state of grace, motoric conflict would follow — to swallow or not to swallow. Such an event would require a name, and anguish was ready-made.

5. The German *Angst*, like the Old French anguisse, is traced back to the Latin *angustus*, "a tightening or pressing together." The semantics of *Angst* have apparently gone through the same development as anxiety but without the orthographic changes.

6. I am indebted to James Kulik for this illustration.

7. One should not draw the inference that all persons under cognitive strain complain of psychophysiological disturbances. The cognitive strain may be eased through various adaptive techniques before prolonged or intense organismic involvement occurs. See Sarbin (1962).

8. In a more detailed account of the present argument, I would also include a discussion of the location of oneself in an explanatory or cosmological ecology. Here the person attempts to locate himself in terms of theoretical structures by answering the question *Why?* In order to do this, he must have acquired a set of theoretical constructs which serve to order events in ways satisfactory to him, eg, force, magnetism, elan vital, libido, phlogistine, lunar attractions, etc. In cognitive theory these constructs, in principle, are no different from the answers given to questions arising from attempts to place oneself in the transcendental ecology. Depending upon one's theoretical purposes, the cosmological ecology might include both transcendental objects and hypothetical explanatory entities. (In the context of clinical inference, this point is discussed in Sarbin, Taft, and Bailey, 1960.)

9. The interested reader will find support for the rejection of mentalism in psychology in G. Ryle, *The Concept of Mind*, 1949.

Synectics

Eugene Raudsepp

One of the more promising methods of promoting creativity in problem solving to emerge in recent years is Synectics. This technique has produced many good inventions, and it also works remarkably well on complex, abstract problems.

The theory of Synectics maintains that people are more creative if they have insight into the psychological processes by which they operate and accept and understand the importance of the "non-rational" aspects of creativity.

The Synectics procedure has been developed "as a deliberate imitation of the way an individual's mind works when he is working at his best," according to George M. Prince, president of Synectics Inc. He further explains that the Synectics procedure "compresses this work — especially the speculative and incubative phases — into a much shorter time span, forcing ideas and associations up for consideration, rather than waiting for them to arise fortuitously."

The objective of a Synectics training course is to increase the existing creative capacity of each participant through: developing a greater understanding of the creative thought processes; improving ability, consciously and deliberately, to make use of the creative mechanism; and developing the capacity to produce better solutions to problems.

TEN PRINCIPLES ESSENTIAL TO
CREATIVE PROBLEM SOLVING

1. Proceed on the assumption that things are possible.
2. Isolate fixed ideas and overcome them.
3. Do not search for solutions, but for new ways to view the problem.

4. Seize on tentative, half-formed possibilities.
5. Recognize that new ideas (one's own as well as others') are fragile, and listen positively to them.
6. Entertain the apparently unthinkable.
7. Articulate the apparently unspeakable.
8. Defer conclusions until a number of variables has been floated.
9. Keep track (by means of brief notation) of the process.
10. Enjoy it!

The Synectics procedures were developed through the aid of the tape recorder. Hundreds of meetings of different groups of people (usually from five to seven) were analyzed, and clues to the kinds of thinking that produce new ideas were documented. Experiments with various procedures finally enabled the Synectics group to come up with various operational mechanisms that have proved most productive.

The crux of the Synectics method is the repeated use of analogies which provide novel contexts for approaching a problem with a fresh outlook. Study of the thought processes of highly creative people has shown that they have the ability to see problems in new and previously unthought of ways. Capitalizing on this fact, the Synectics process deliberately cultivates and makes use of the seemingly irrelevant.

OPERATIONAL MECHANISMS

The Synectics method involves two basic approaches to problem solving: *Making-the-Strange-Familiar* and *Making-the-Familiar-Strange.*

Making-the-Strange-Familiar: This is the analytical phase which plumbs the ramifications and the fundamentals of the problem to get to the heart of it. Making the strange familiar is essentially congenial to the natural tendency of the mind. When presented with a problem or with something unfamiliar, our natural tendency is to convert it, through analysis and comparison with previously consolidated information and data, into manageable familiarity.

The three basic procedures employed in making the strange familiar are: *Analysis, Generalization,* and *Model-seeking.* Analysis involves the breaking down of the complexity into its component parts (seeing the forest more clearly by identifying the individual trees). Generalization is the process by which we identify significant patterns among the parts. By Model-seeking we facilitate the formulation of generalizations.

While analysis — the making the strange familiar — is, of course, the necessary part of creative problem solving, it is full of pitfalls. Often it involves mere concentration on details, which become ends in themselves, leading one into a variety of superficial solutions. Analysis in itself does not lead one into a fresh viewpoint, a new way of looking at the problem. For this the approach of Making-the-Familiar-Strange is necessary.

Making-the-Familiar-Strange: Through deliberate distortion, inversion, or transportation, the everyday habitual ways of looking at things are rendered strange. It is not merely a search for the bizarre or out-of-the-way, it is a conscious attempt to achieve a new look at the "familiar world," to transpose both our usual ways of perceiving and our habitual expectations about how we or the world will behave.

Synectics emphasizes the importance of viewpoints and claims that a usefully strange viewpoint can suggest several different potential solutions. While the traditional problem-solving procedures seek solutions, Synectics seeks new viewpoints, using them as springboards to solutions.

'METHOD' THINKING

Synectics has identified three mechanisms for making the familiar strange: *Personal Analogy; Direct Analogy;* and *Symbolic Analogy.*

Personal Analogy: In Synectics, Personal Analogy involves using one's own highly personal emotions, feelings and characteristics for obtaining insight into purely technological problems. George M. Prince explains it: "One identifies oneself with a purely nonhuman entity which figures in the problem, investing it with one's own vitality, speculating on how that THING would 'feel' and act in the problem situation. The device has proven an invaluable tool for making-the-familiar-strange. Personal identification with the elements of a problem releases the individual from viewing the problem in terms of its previously analyzed elements."

Application of Personal Analogy

A Synectics group had been attacking the problem of inventing a new and inexpensive constant speed mechanism. The problem: how to run a shaft at input speeds varying from

400 to 4,000 rpm so that the power takeoff end of this shaft always turns at 400. Since many competent engineers had tried to solve this constant speed problem, there was little hope for arriving at anything elegant unless a totally new viewpoint were gained. A mechansim for making this familiar problem strange was Personal Analogy. A sketch was drawn on the blackboard showing a box with a shaft entering and going out. The entering shaft was labelled "400 to 4,000"; the exiting shaft was labelled "400 constant." One after the other, each member of the group 'entered' the box and attempted to effect with his own body the constant speed required. Here are some excerpts from the recorded session in response to the questions: "You're in the box — how do you feel? What do you do?"

Okay, I'm in the black box. I grab the in-shaft with one hand and grab the out-shaft with the other. I let the in-shaft slip when I think it's going too fast so that the out-shaft will stay constant. . . .

Well, my hands are getting . . . too hot to hold I guess . . . at least one hand, that is . . . the one that's acting like a clutch . . . slipping.

. . . I'm in the box and I am trying to be a governor . . . to be a feedback system . . . built in . . . let's see, if I grab the out-shaft with my hands . . . and let's say there's a plate on the in-shaft so that my feet can press against it . . . I put my feet way out in the periphery of the plate and . . . what I would like is for my feet to get smaller as the speed of the in-shaft increases because then the friction would be reduced and I would hold on to the out-shaft for dear life and its speed might remain constant. . . . The faster the in-shaft went the smaller my feet would become so that the driving force would stay the same.

The above analogies not only increase the understanding of the problem, but they can also suggest potential avenues of solution.

Direct Analogy: This mechanism is used in Synectics to compare parallel facts, knowledge, or technology. The procedure entails searching one's experiences and knowledge to marshal phenomena that have some similar relationships with the problem at hand. However, exact comparisons, or comparisons with subject matter too close to the problem are useless for the purpose of making-the-familiar-strange. For example, comparing an organ with a piano is too close a parallel to evoke new viewpoints; comparing it with a typewriter might be productive of more intriguing notions.

Marc Isambard Brunel discovered a method for underwater construction by watching a shipworm tunnelling into a timber. The worm constructed a tube for itself as it moved forward, and the classical notion of caissons arose — by Direct Analogy. Alexander Graham Bell recalled, "It struck me that the bones of the human ear were very massive indeed, as compared with the delicate thin membrane that operated them, and the thought occurred that if a membrane so delicate could move bones so relatively massive, why should not a thicker and stouter piece of membrane move my piece of steel. And the telephone was conceived."

Synectics believes that, in the case of technical problems, analogies drawn from nature and from other sciences are effective. Particularly effective in terms of creating constructive new viewpoints are analogies drawn from the organic world. Comparisons from different areas of exact science, on the other hand, tend to be too close.

Application of Direct Analogy

A Synectics group was attempting to solve the problem of how to invent a new kind of roof which would be more actively serviceable than traditional roofs. Analysis of the problem indicated that there might be an economic advantage in having a roof white in the summer and black in winter. The white roof would reflect the sun's rays in summer so that the cost of air conditioning could be reduced. The black roof would absorb heat in winter so that the cost of heating could be minimized. The following are some Direct Analogy examples from the session on this problem, which started with the question: "What in nature changes color?"

A weasel — white in winter, brown in summer; camouflage. It's not voluntary and the weasel changes color only twice a year. I think our roof should change color with the heat of the sun. There are hot days in the spring and fall . . . cold ones too.

A flounder is light in color if he is over white sand, then he turns dark if he lands on black sand. This changing is partly voluntary and partly nonvoluntary where a reflex action automatically adapts to the surrounding conditions. This is how the switching works: in the deepest layer of its skin are black-pigmented chromatophores — balls of color. When these are pushed toward the surface the flounder is covered with black spots so that he looks black, like an impressionistic painting where a whole bunch of little dabs of paint give the appearance of total covering. Only when you get up close to a Seurat can you see the little atomistic dabs. When the black pigment withdraws to the bottom of these chromatophores, then the flounder appears light colored.

Analysis: Let's compare the flounder analogy with the roof problem. Let's say we make up a roofing material that's black, but buried in the black stuff are little white plastic balls. When the sun comes out and the roof gets hot, the little white balls expand according to Boyle's law. They pop through the black roofing vehicle. Now the roof is white, impressionistically white that is. Just like the flounder, only with reverse english. Is it the black pigmented part of the chromatophores that come to the surface of the flounder's skin? OK, in our roof it will be the white pigmented plastic balls that come to the surface when the roof gets hot. There are many ways to think about this . . .

The knowledge of zoology imparted was not childlike or naive. The flounder analogy was backed up by technical insight without which no new viewpoint would have been possible.

Over a period of years Synectics research has observed that perhaps the richest source of Direct Analogy is biology. This is because the language of biology lacks a mystifying terminology, and the organic aspect of biology brings out analogies which breathe life into problems that are stiff and rigidly quantitative.

C. F. Kettering made use of Direct Analogy when tetraethyl lead was invented. As T. A. Boyd writes in his *Biography of C. F. Kettering:*

"Speculating then on why kerosene knocked worse than gasoline, as it was known to do, the two men reasoned that it might be because kerosene did not vaporize as readily as gasoline. They recalled that the wild flower, the trailing arbutus, with its red-backed leaves, blooms early in spring, even under the snow. If only kerosene were dyed red, they speculated, it might − like the leaves of the trailing arbutus − absorb heat faster, and so vaporize quickly enough to burn in the engine like gasoline."

Symbolic Analogy: Symbolic Analogy is defined by Synectics as "a highly compressed, almost poetic, statement of the implications of a key word selected from the Problem-As-Understood or having some connection with the problem."

George M. Prince illustrates the mechanism of Symbolic Analogy this way:

The procedure is to select the key word and ask yourself (or a member of your group) for the essence of its meaning to you. Empathize or feel for the important connotations of the word. Then try to put those feelings into one or two words. The more general or all-encompassing these words are, the more potentially useful in suggesting areas for speculation. Straight definitions are not useful because they are low level descriptions of a one-to-one type. They give little opportunity to search for associations. In a Synectics session directed toward detecting the presence of an unwanted flame in a piece of sophisticated hardware, the question was asked: "What is the essence of flameness?"

A flame is ghostly and seems insubstantial but is very much there . . . it's a ghostly thereness. ['Ghostly thereness' is the Symbolic Analogy.]

It's ghostly because it wavers and doesn't seem to have much substance but if you put your finger in its territory it sure is there.

It really does occupy that space and nothing else can. It's a ghost with a shell. . . .

Or a skin, or a wall . . . a ghostly wall. (Symbolic Analogy.)

Considering a flame as a ghostly wall led to some rewarding lines of speculation.

Some typical Symbolic Analogies follow (key words to which the analogies apply are in the left-hand column).

Ratchet	Dependable intermittency
Viscosity	Hesitant displacement
Solidity	Enforced togetherness
Forest fire	Progressive ingestion
Machine-gun burst	Connected pauses
Target	Focussed desire
Mixture	Balanced confusion
Multitude	Discreet infinity
Acid	Impure aggressor
Receptivity	Involuntary willingness

Symbolic Analogies are the toughest to create. Compressing into a single meaningful phrase the crucial essence of a subject takes hard work and effort. However, people trained in the use of Synectics claim that Symbolic Analogy more often leads to conceptual breakthroughs than any of the other mechanisms described. The "useful strangeness" that symbolic analogy imparts to familiar objects and concepts transcends those that can·be obtained by the use of either Personal or Direct Analogy.

In actual Synectics use, the above mechanisms usually overlap. In developing a good Symbolic Analogy, for example, one may start with a Direct Analogy.

The analogical mechanisms are the most important part of the Synectics method, although they tend to appear often ambiguous and seemingly irrelevant. George M. Prince defends the ambiguity this way: "It is this very ambiguity on which Synectics depends for making-the-familiar-strange. But the analogies must be sought within an ordered framework if they are to be efficient. And they must be 'force-fitted' to the problem if they are to be effective. Through the strain of this new fit the problem is stretched and pulled and refocussed in order that it may be seen in a nèw way. If no deliberate attempt is made to find relevance in apparent irrelevance, then one analogy can merely lead to another and another, and potentially fruitful viewpoints will be by-passed."

To impose a disciplined *framework* on the generation, development, and use of analogical mechanisms, a Flow Chart has been developed. All sessions should follow this chart.

SYNECTICS FLOW CHART
Sessions should be constructed according to this plan.
A. PAG (Problem-as-Given)
    A general statement of the problem to be solved.
B. Analysis and discussion to make the strange problem familiar
C. Purge of immediate solutions.
D. PAU (Problem-as-Understood)
    An element or aspect of the problem upon which to concentrate.
E. EQ (Evocative Question)
    A question that forces an analogical answer.
    ANALOGY GENERATION
    Direct Analogy
        or
    Personal Analogy
        or
    Symbolic Analogy

F. ANALOGY DEVELOPMENT

Playing with the analogy to understand all of its implications.

G. ANALOGY USE

Application of this understanding to the PAU (or PAG) to see if a new viewpoint can be developed.

H. There are now several alternative courses.

1. If there is a new viewpoint it should be developed as far as possible and then evaluated.

2. If there is no new viewpoint, another "excursion" is begun to make-the-familiar-strange:

a. Make more analogies to the same EQ and repeat F and G

or

b. Return to the PAU, use a new EQ and repeat F and G

or

c. If the work in G reveals a new aspect to the problem, state this as a new PAU and repeat E, F, and G.

PROBLEM DEFINITION IS CRITICAL

It is important to recognize that problem statement significantly influences the way the problem will be approached. Consequently, following the PAG (Problem-As-Given) statement, there is an analytical phase leading the group to decide on which formulation of the problem is going to be the first subject of attack. This statement is called the PAU (Problem-As-Understood).

The analytical stage from PAG to PAU usually accomplishes a number of purposes: it makes the strange familiar to those participants in the group who are not familiar with the problem and its background; it is used to elicit and nullify those immediate solution possibilities which inevitably occur to group members but which rarely prove adequate. It is held essential that all members of the group purge themselves of the "premature" solutions as they arise, for an individual's constructive participation in the session is lost as long as he dwells on his first solution possibility.

The first PAU serves merely as a common starting point, judged by the group as a potentially fruitful topic to concentrate upon. The PAU is frequently restated, and it is not uncommon for the group to discover that the real heart of the problem lies elsewhere than in the first definition by the PAG.

In the Synectics process, thinking oscillates in an orderly fashion between analysis and analogy, between making-the-strange-familiar, and making-the-familiar-strange. Analogies permit the group to deliberately distort the "image" of the problem, to gain a new look at it, after which it is allowed to come back into focus.

THE GROUP LEADER'S ROLE

The important decision of which analogical route the group is to take rests on the leader. He makes this decision by the criterion of "constructive psychological strain." With a mechanical problem, for example, he would look for biological models. With people-oriented problems, he might seek analogies from the exact sciences. The Synectics groups have found that the more concrete the problem, the greater is the likelihood that symbolic analogy will be fruitful.

It is the leader's responsibility to evoke analogical responses by means of so-called Evocative Questions, which form the bridge between the analysis and analogy. The leader specifies which type of analogy he wants (direct, personal, or symbolic), and he usually singles out the response from one particular group member. A good leader soon learns that each group member ususally has greater facility with one kind of analogy than the others, and the leader captializes on that knowledge.

After the analogy has emerged, the group devotes all its attention to it and defers, for the time being, all conscious thought of the problem-as-given. In the subconscious, however, the problem-as-given acts as a guide to signal to the group members whenever a useful viewpoint implied by the analogies is articulated.

A period of analogy development ensues, during which time all the details of the analogy are analyzed and the important details emphasized. If the group fails to articulate a useful connection between the problem-as-understood (PAU) and the analogy, the leader will direct them to try a "force-fitting" connection, making sure that all potential viewpoints from the analogy are considered.

If the analogy succeeds in illuminating the problem-as-understood, a viewpoint is gained and an attempt is made to apply it to the problem-as-given (PAG) to see whether it answers all the parameters of the problem. If it fails in this, then a new problem-as-understood (PAU) is stated. This statement reflects the questions that were left unanswered or the difficulties that were encountered.

If the analogy fails to move even the new problem-as-understood (PAU) closer to solution, then a new analogical exercise is required.

The Synectics process involves the whole man, both his subjective and objective experience, and his expertise.

Although the Synectics group sessions are conducted by a leader, the leader's functions are different from what is usually meant by the term. The Synectics leader never judges or passes on the merits of a contribution. Neither does he act as a moderator or a chairman. His major function is to see to it that the problem investigation stays within the confines of the flow chart. He also insures the most efficient generation, development, and use of analogies. In a sense, his role often is that of merely filling in the gaps "between speeches," and of keeping track of the progress on boards or easel pads that all participants can review.

Another important quality in a leader, according to William J. J. Gordon, is "an almost pathological optimism supporting a refusal to give up." As Gordon points out, "Solutions to many problems remain undiscovered because inventors ran out of creative energy just when they were on the brink. Of course, it is impossible to know where the brink is, but in the case of all problems there exist certain walls which define the line where others have surrendered. It is just when we strike these seemingly impenetrable bastions that we tend toward despair, like others before us . . . and it is just then that we are on the verge of solution."

SETTING UP A SYNECTICS GROUP

One factor that is essential to the success of the Synectics group is diversity. The five to seven individuals selected for the group should represent differing backgrounds, training, and experience in the company. The first benefit to be gained from diversity of backgrounds and training is that each member of the group quite naturally will view each problem from a different viewpoint. It is an extremely difficult task for an individual to "step back," so to speak, from a deep understanding of, or familiarity with, a problem in order to look at it afresh. A group of individuals with diverse backgrounds can do this much more readily. The second important benefit to be gained from diversity of background and training is the variety of knowledge that is brought to bear on a problem. "The possibilities of innovation are greatest in the no-man's-land which separates specialties, rather than in the well-trodden areas within specific fields," according to Dean L. Gitter.

Gitter feels that companies interested in establishing Synectics groups should assemble a group of men who have worked in various areas of the company's activities: production, research, finance, sales, development, etc. This makes it possible to maximize the knowledge of the company's needs, opportunities, and attidues and break through the arbitrary barriers that inevitably exist between the various divisions and departments of a corporation. Gitter says, "If we combine, in one group, knowledge of possibilities extant in the marketplace, basic research knowledge which has yet to be capitalized on, practical abilities to unite these poles, and an overall commitment to get the job done, then the possibility exists for synthesizing both an inventor and entrepreneur out of the individuals possessing these skills."

The groups that receive Synectics training are exposed to a variety of problems which are usually supplied by management. They must be of immediate importance to the company in order to elicit the group's interest and dedication. Ideally, the problems should also be of sufficient potential profitability to assuage management's concern with the expenditures of time and energies.

Dean L. Gitter feels that a few problems that are initially attacked should lend themselves to short-range implementation and measurable results. This gives the group a sense of achievement and a faith in the newly learned modus operandi of Synectics. Interestingly enough, one of the early problem solutions is also used as a "scapegoat." "We have found it useful," explains Gitter, "to deliberately sacrifice one of the group's early inventions, to send it out into the organization and observe the direction from which the arrows come to shoot it down, and the techniques the hunters use to do it. In watching this slaughter, the group learns many ways in which to improve future performance; members develop a heightened sense of reliance they must place on each other and the group;

the group begins to evolve a set of commando tactics for coping with opposition. Above all, it begins to find its own sense of style and the satisfaction which comes from commitment. They also learn that no group of six individuals can hope to take an invention all the way from conception to the marketplace on its own — they must constructively involve the rest of the organization."

* *

Synectics Inc., Cambridge, Mass., is engaged primarily in four areas of endeavor: inventing products and processes for sale or license to industry; acting as consultants on specific problems with client companies; teaching the Synectics method of problem solving to groups of industrial and business personnel; and continuing research into the creative process.

Employees of a number of blue-chip American industries have participated in Synectics courses. Many of these companies have also submitted problems for Synectics Inc. to solve, and several have established operating Synectics groups. Although the method has been applied successfully to administration, marketing, personnel management, production, research, cost reduction, new product application, and process improvement, the greatest demand for training has been in the area of new product development.

The founder of the company, William J. J. Gordon, holds more than 50 patents. He is also the author of a book entitled, *Synectics: The Development of Creative Capacity.*

Why use Synectics? Research, according to Dean L. Gitter, vice president of the company, has revealed these two facts:

- The commodity called "creativity" is much more universally distributed among the population than is usually supposed.
- The creative habit can be reawakened in people who seem to have lost it and strengthened in people who regularly display it.

* *

1. "Forcing Ideas with Synectics . . . a creative approach to problem solving." Reprinted from *Machine Design* Oct. 16, 1969. Copyright, 1969, by The Penton Publishing Company, Cleveland, Ohio.

Visual-Verbal Rhetoric

Gui Bonsiepe

Rhetoric has fallen not so much into disrepute as into virtual oblivion. It has come down to us from ancient times with an aura of antiquity about it that makes it seem, at first sight, unsuited to handling the message of the advertiser, which is the rhetoric of the modern age. Yet it can be shown that a modern system of rhetoric might be a useful descriptive and analytical tool for dealing with the phenomena of advertising. To explain how is the aim of this article.

The ancient Greeks divided rhetoric (the art of eloquence) into three parts: the political, the legal, and the religious. It was primarily the politicians, lawyers, and priests who were adepts in rhetoric, since it was their business to use speech to work on their public. Their object was to obtain a definite decision (on a campaign of war); to implant an opinion (concerning the prisoner at the bar); to evoke a mood (in a religious ceremony). The domain of rhetoric is the domain of logomachy, the war of words.

Rhetoric divides into two kinds: one is concerned with the use of persuasive means (rhetorica utens) and the other with description and analysis (rhetorica docens). Practice and theory are closely linked in rhetoric. It is generally defined as the art of persuasion, or the study of the means of persuasion. The aim of rhetoric is primarily to shape opinions, to determine the attitude of other people, or to influence their actions. Where force rules, there is no need of rhetoric. As Burke says (in "A Rhetoric of Motives," N.Y., 1955), "It is directed to a man only in so far as he is *free*. . . . Insofar as he *must* do something, rhetoric is superfluous."

These conditions of choice are fulfilled by the situation on a competitive market where various wares come together. The consumer is given a wide range of choice among goods and services, and it becomes desirable to influence him in the selection he makes. This is the function of advertising. And so a new partner joins the classical triad of politics, justice, and religion in the domain of rhetoric; and that is marketing.

Of the listing of rhetorical processes there is no end. Shades of meaning have been set down with precision. Textbooks of rhetoric (and they are still textbooks of classical rhetoric) are as notable for their abundance of fine-spun distinctions as for their uncritical acceptance of traditional classifications. A terminology suited to Latin and Greek makes it difficult to use these concepts; rhetoric is weighed down by more than two thousand years of ballast. The time has come to bring it up to date with the aid of semiotics (a general theory of signs and symbols). For, apart from inconsistencies in the concepts it uses, classical rhetoric (which deals purely with language) is no longer adequate for describing and analyzing rhetorical phenomena in which verbal *and visual* signs, i.e. word and picture, are allied. Here the practice of rhetoric has far outrun its theory.

If one thinks of the unending spate of posters, advertisements, films, and television spots turned out by an industrial society with all the facilities of the communications industry at its command, and compares it with the very sporadic efforts made to throw light on the rhetorical aspects of this information, the discrepancy stares one in the face.

The five main sections of classical rhetoric can be reduced to only one useful for the analysis of advertising information: the third, covering the linguistic and stylistic formulation of the material. The rules for collecting, arranging, memorizing, and speaking, can be largely ignored. The stylistic aspects of rhetoric appear primarily as rhetorical figures, which can be defined (after Quintilian) as "the art of saying something in a new form" or (after Burke) as "changing the meaning or application of words in order to give the speech greater suavity, vitality and impact." According to classical theory, the essence of a rhetorical figure consists in a departure from normal speech usage, for the purpose of making the message more effective.

These figures fall into two classes: (1) word figures, which work with the meaning of words or the position of words in the sentence; and (2) idea figures, which work with the shaping and organization of information. The terminology of semiotics makes it easier to sort out these figures. Starting from the fact that there are two aspects to every sign, namely its shape and its meaning, we arrive at two basic types of rhetorical figure; for such a figure can operate through the shape of the sign or through its meaning. If we consider the shape, we are in the dimension of syntax. If we consider the meaning — or relata, to use the semiotic term — we are in the dimension of semantics. (Relatum is a term embracing everything a sign stands for; its sub-classes are the things designated, the things denoted, and the things signified. The technical words for these are designata, denotata, and significata.) Using this classification, it follows that the two classes of rhetorical figure are the syntactic and the semantic. A figure is syntactic when it operates through the shape of the sign; it is semantic when it operates through the relatum (or referent). In traffic signs, we find that contours, colors and sign arrangements belong to the syntactic dimensions, and the meanings belong to the semantic.

Sifting and simplifying the ultrafine distinctions of classical rhetoric, we can catalogue the verbal rhetorical figures thus:

I. SYNTACTIC FIGURES

A. Transpositive figures (departure from normal word order)

1. Apposition (expalantory insertions)

2. Atomization (treating dependent parts of a sentence as independent)

3. Parenthesis (enclosing one sentence in another)

4. Reversion or anastrophe (dislocation of a word for emphasis)

B. Privative figures (omission of words)

1. Ellipsis (leaving out words which can be supplied from the context) .

C. Repetitive figures

1. Alliteration (repeating an initial letter or sound)

2. Isophony (repeating sounds of similar words, or parts of words, in a series)

3. Parallelism (repeating the same rhythm in successive clauses or sentences)

4. Repetition (repeating a word in various positions)

II. SEMANTIC FIGURES

A. Contrary figures (based on the union of opposite relata)

1. Antithesis (confrontation in a sentence of parts having opposite meanings)

2. Exadversion (assertion by a double negative)

3. Conciliation (coupling of contradictory relata)

B. Comparative figures (based on comparisons between the relata)

1. Gradation (words in an ascending order of forcefulness)

2. Hyperbole (exaggeration)

3. Metaphor (transfer of a word to another field of application in such a way that a similarity of any kind between the two fields is assumed and given expression)

4. Understatement

C. Substitutive figures (based on replacement of the relata)

1. Metonymy (replacement of one sign by another, the relata of both being in a real relationship)

2. Synecdoche (a special case of metonymy: replacement of one sign by another, the relata of both being in a quantitative relationship)

III. PRAGMATIC FIGURES

A. Fictitious dialogue (speaker asks and answers himself)

B. Direct speech

C. Conversion of an objection into an argument in one's own favor

D. Asteism (irrelevant replies to a question or argument)

With the aid of these definitions from the art of rhetoric, advertising copy can be analyzed and described in terms of its rhetorical characteristics. In this way, its persuasive structure can be brought to light.

It is the usage among philosophers of language to contrast persuasion with information, opinion shaping with documentation and instruction, and everyday speech with scientific language. In the eyes of orthodox representative of a purified and unambiguous language, rhetoric is merely a handbook of verbal tricks, unworthy of the true scientist. In reply to this, the champions of rhetoric argue that the systematic ambiguity of linguistic signs is an inevitable consequence of the power of language, and is an indispensable part of the means of human communication. In thrashing out the theoretical question whether there can or cannot be any communication without rhetoric, the arguments seem to favor the latter alternative. The only examples of simple, dehydrated information, innocent of all taint of rhetoric, that come readily to hand are such things as logarithm tables, timetables, and telephone books. Fortunately communication is not limited to this; informative assertions are interlarded with rhetoric to a greater or lesser degree. If they were not, communication would die of sheer inanition.

"Pure" information exists for the designer only in arid abstraction. As soon as he begins to give it concrete shape, the process of rhetorical infiltration begins. It would seem that many designers — blinded by their effort to impart objective information (whatever that may mean) — simply will not face this fact. They cannot reconcile themselves to the idea that advertising is *addressed* information, and that its informative content is often secondary if it plays any role at all.

It is hard not to feel a little sympathy for this view, mistaken though it may be. It is the expression of a certain unease, a dissatisfaction with the role of the visual designer, felt in our competitive society, where his abilities are often wasted on the mere representation of the imaginary qualities of goods and services. And this representation often strikes a grandiloquent note in blatant contrast to the triviality and banality of the product offered. The prescribed, euphoric superlative is humbug. It is just as much humbug as "objective" information in advertising which is ashamed of its promotional purpose and tries to dissemble itself.

Once the point is yielded that there are various grades of rhetorical infiltration, then the question arises how these different grades can be assessed in terms of quantity. Mensuration and numerical data are the order of the day. They parade as the proud achievements of science. Despite a certain suspicion of figure-fetishism, which will accept new knowledge on the sole condition that it is in numerical terms, we can sketch out a simple possibility for measuring the rhetorical content of a text. In measurements one must keep to the ascertainable. And what is ascertainable in a text is the number of rhetorical figures of various kinds which it contains. The ratio of rhetorical figures to normal sentences in advertising copy is an index of its persuasiveness. If ten rhetorical figures and five normal sentences appear in a text, it may be said to have a persuasion grade of 2. What persuasion is, is not specified. It is not even defined. All that is given is the data needed to measure what is called persuasiveness.

Verbal rhetoric paves the way to visual rhetoric. As we said before, classical rhetoric was confined to language. But most posters, advertisements, films, and television spots contain linguistic and non-linguistic signs side by side, and these signs are not independent, but interact closely. So it makes good sense to ask about typical picture/word combinations, typical sign relations, and visual/verbal rhetorical figures.

Visual rhetoric is still virgin territory. In what follows we shall make some tentative efforts to explore this new country. Our discussion is based mainly on interpretations of the analysis of a series of advertisements.

Taking the conclusions of verbal rhetoric as a guide, we dissected out figures having exclusive reference to the interplay of word and picture. The terms of verbal rhetoric were used to designate the concepts of this new rhetoric. New concepts were introduced where necessary. In this first approach, the visual/verbal figures were simply noted. The work of classifying and systematizing them still remains to be done.

To define a visual/verbal figure, it is no longer enough to apply the criterion of the "departure from normal usage" as in verbal figures; for it cannot be established what relations between verbal and visual signs form the standard from which one can depart. It would, therefore, seem more appropriate for purposes of definition to fall back upon the possible interactions already inherent in the signs. Thus a visual/verbal rhetorical figure is a combination of two types of sign whose effectiveness in communication depends on the tension between their semantic characteristics. The signs no longer simply add up, but rather operate in cumulative reciprocal relations.

Illustrations are given reproduced from Ulm 14/15/16 which is the Journal of the Ulm School for Design.

1. Visual/verbal comparison (a comparison that starts with verbal signs and is continued with visual signs).

Advertisement: Young & Rubicam

The "sharp ideas" expressed verbally are represented by the sharpened pencil. The sameness of the advertisements from which an effective advertisement stands out is illustrated by the uniform row of unsharpened (= ineffective) pencils.

2. Visual/verbal analogy (a relatum expressed verbally is paralleled by a similar relatum expressed visually).

Advertisement: Esso

"Refuel anywhere." The refuelling of cars is illustrated by the analogy of the feeding hummingbird.

3. Visual/verbal metonymy (a relatum indicated by verbal signs is visualized by signs in a real relationship to the verbal relatum; e.g. cause instead of effect, tool instead of activity, producer instead of product).

Advertisement: Esso

"Be precise!" The imperative expressed verbally is visualized by the tool (a micrometer) for carrying it out.

4. Visual synecdoche (a relatum expressed verbally is visualized by a part representing the whole, or vice-versa).

Advertisement: Kardex

"You find Kardex in the most unlikely places." The baby is a visual sign standing for the whole nursery, and for the whole class of "unlikely places".

5. Visual substitution (one visual sign replaced by another because of its formal characteristics).

Advertisement: Univac

"Geizkragen" ("Greedy-collar" = "skinflint").

The metaphorical word is illustrated by a punch card bent to look like a collar.

6. Visual/verbal parallelism (visual and verbal signs representing the same relatum).

Advertisement: VW

"You never run out of air." The abundance of air suggested verbally is visualized by an inserted area of light grey.

7. Associative mediation (one verbal sign out of a series is illustrated by a series of visual signs, which lead, in turn, to another relatum of the verbal signs).

Advertisement: Smirnoff Vodka

"Take a holiday from everyday drinks!"

The verbal element "holidays" is singled out of the series and illustrated by means of an open porthole, sunset, and a calm sea. Thus vodka and holidays are linked together.

1. Reprinted from *Dot Zero* (New York) 2 (1967) 37-42. (All pictures and several examples omitted.)

Models and Mystery

Ian T. Ramsey

On the view I am putting forward a metaphor would always be a signpost to some disclosure, some insight and inspiration, from which it takes its rise. Metaphors would be born in, and thereafter intended to evoke, a disclosure associated with a tangential meeting of two diverse contexts,[2] e.g. the connecting of old age with autumn, a religious leader with light, the head of a college with a carved statue, libraries with powerhouses. From this tangential meeting between contexts, and as currency for the disclosure which that meeting evokes, discourse is then developed metaphorically when the second language infiltrates into the first in the most selective and subtle way. What I am saying is that the metaphorical expression 'A is B' arises in a disclosure where languages A and B meet tangentially, touching at a point, or rather at two coincident points. Hence, the 'is' of a metaphor has to be understood as a claim that (i) A and B in contact have generated a disclosure revealing some object and (ii) what it is that has been disclosed demands discourse which infiltrates B into A. In this way we would explicate, for example, 'Electricity *is* flowing in the wire'; 'Light *is* a wave motion'; 'Jesus *is* the Messiah'. In each case the copula 'is' points to a disclosure whose object brings with it the possibility and need of endless novelty in metaphorical talking. Indeed I suggest that it is the built-in possibility of endless novelty, in virtue of which metaphors point to the mystery and elusiveness of what has been disclosed. In fact what some[3] would call a mere eccentricity of language I have called a tangential meeting, and my point is that such eccentricity is not to be despised for its irregularity but welcomed for its enrichment, welcomed for the mystery to which it points, mystery because its explication is

163

an endless unravelling. There is no prior bound to the development of metaphorical discourse; nor are there any intrinsic limits to the transaction and interchange between contexts which a metaphor makes possible. A metaphor holds together two contexts in such a way as to generate an unspecifiable number of articulation possibilities. There is thus a tangential connexion between the head of an Oxford College and the figurehead of a ship; the metaphor is born in insight and this leads to discourse of the kind we began to formulate above. Again, there is tangential connexion between electricity and flowing water; here, too, is a metaphor born in insight leading to possibilities of discourse when we speak of a current or electricity flowing in a wire and so on. Yet again, there is a tangential connexion between talk about Jesus and talk about the Messiah; here too is a metaphor born in insight, and it leads to all kinds of discourse possibilities. Metaphors then are not just link devices between different contexts. They are necessarily grounded in inspiration.

Generalizing, we may say that metaphorical expressions occur when two situations strike us in such a way as to reveal what includes them but is no mere combination of them both. Metaphors and models, both enabling us to be articulate about an insight, are thus the basic currency for mystery, and we can spend our lives elucidating ever more faithfully the mystery in which metaphors and models are born.

*　　*　　*　　*　　*　　*　　*

These models may lead us to a disclosure of God in Christ. The same will be true of all the understandings of the universe and of society with which each discipline can provide us. Theology can lead each subject to the wonder and insight which matches mystery, as and when it allows that subject to help it to be articulate. Theology will never direct, but in fellowship with other disciplines will seek for a better understanding of the mystery to which it must always point.

I would now like to bring these lectures to an end by a brief word on the significance of what I have been saying for our contemporary social life, and for the concept of a university in particular.

My overall point might be expressed by saying that I have emphasized the limitations and deceptive attractions of descriptive language. Such pictorial language may undoubtedly have some uses and some important uses. But let us not forget that those who use a language match the language they use. For language is integrated with its speaker in a verbal and non-verbal context. If in fact anyone thought that descriptive language, sponsoring pictorial models, was the whole story, they would by that very confusion be confessing themselves to be routine-bound morons, flotsam and jetsam in a fact-bound existence, lacking spontaneity of behaviour, sensitivity, imagination, 'the personal touch' — indeed, lacking all that is distinctively personal. On the other hand, I have argued for the wide significance over the whole field of human knowledge of insight and disclosures, to which models (of the reliable kind) and metaphors, and what are by descriptive standards the most eccentric of our words and phrases, bear witness. It is in using these words that we are most characteristically persons, rather than mere organisms or even social units. In this sense we realize our transcendence, and the universe which discloses itself to us is similarly, by descriptive standards, 'mysterious' and likewise transcendent. What is not verbally odd is void of disclosure power; but words can be found in using which the universe and ourselves come alive together in a cosmic disclosure.

Our danger today is that we may become routine-bound in our performances. It may be a colourful routine and an affluent routine, and it is certainly none the worse for being an affluent routine. But it is routine nevertheless, and from the philosopher's point of view our major problem is to discover anew, in novel patterns of commerce and industry, in all upheavals of rapid social change, occasions of inspiration and disclosure. Our major problem today is to discover new occasions of disclosure in an affluent society. Then, and only then, will maids and matrons, management and labour, plumbers and professors, find a creative satisfaction in their work; only then will they be persons.

In every way we must resist attempts to make men and cultures conform to a cut and dried language which would strangle all creative life. We have to recapture for our affluent society the kind of vision which fired those early religious leaders of the British labour movement, or, to show my political neutrality, which fired those empire-builders of a past day who, like John Cabot, gazing on the rocky coast of Newfoundland after days on the Atlantic, found a disclosure in the discovery of new land, and responded with a total devotion. The day comes when politics is no longer a spiritual mission but a professional game, and when Cabot's vision gives way to empire jingoists — when insight and disclosure have been lost. It is then that we can remember that it is the role of the true theology to stir vision, and to remind us of the mysterious. The implication is that in all our present lassitude, as at all other times, the Church must be characterized by a divine discontent. The greatest condemnation of the Church, as of Christian theology, is that it should vegetate in a self-satisfied finality and neglect the vision which stirs.

Let me conclude by coming nearer home — to the implications of what I have said for the concept of a university. On the view I have developed, what will characterize a university — a *studium generale,* a *universitas,* a *collegium* — is the sense of a common devotion, the sense that all the understandings of its different disciplines are the understandings of a mystery common to them all, which in a Christian university will be talked of in specifically Christian terms. The perpetual task of theology within such a university must be to familiarize itself as best it can with the ever-changing models of the various disciplines; to declare the need to work out appropriately new routes to God; as well as to show the way in which traditional phrases and formulae were and are able to be accepted currency for the mystery of which they spoke. If theology may alert other disciplines to the claims of mystery and insight and disclosures, it must learn from other disciplines how to be more and more reliably articulate.

Here is a university as a co-operative venture of understanding, sponsoring a common exploration of problems, where models are always fulfilled in mystery, and mystery is articulated in models; where each academic discipline provides by its own models its own characteristic understanding of a mystery which confronts them all; and where the union of disciplines is to be found in a wonder and insight and worship, which all may share and for whose understanding they all offer their own particular clues. Here is a view of a university, not as a mere arena for power struggles between professional disciplines, still less as a mere setting in which men go about their segregated jobs; here is a university which holds together and harmonizes the technical and the humane, the specialization and the broad perspective, the mind which is analytically critical and the person who is broadly sensitive and sympathetic, which holds together understanding and insight, models and mystery.

What has been my argument in this lecture? Models, like metaphors, enable us, I have said, to be articulate, and both are born in insight. But it is an insight which, viewed as a disclosure, reminds us that in such insight the universe is revealing itself to us. Here we pass beyond Max Black's position, and not least when we see the implications for theology which emerges as a purveyor of insight, a discipline which spotlights and calls attention to those qualifiers which, in all language, will be associated with models if that language is to be fully adequate to its topic. My conclusion was that these views had important implications for such practical topics as those of church unity, the dissatisfactions of an affluent society, and the character of a university.

1. Reprinted from Ian T. Ramsey *Models and Mystery* London: Oxford University Press 1964 "Models and Qualifiers: Understanding and Insight" pp. 52-53, 68-71.

2. Cf. E. Nagel, *The Structure of Science: Problems in the Logic of Scientific Explanation.* On p. 108 he says that metaphors testify to a 'pervasive human talent for finding resemblances between new experiences and familiar facts'. Or, of course, there may be no 'finding'; we may just become aware of such resemblances as they 'strike' us in a disclosure.

3. *E.g.* T. D. Weldon in his *Vocabulary of Politics* (London, Penguin Books, 1953), p. 9: '. . . philosophers have become extremely self-conscious about language. They have come to realize that many of the problems which their predecessors have found insuperable arose not from anything mysterious or inexplicable in the world but from the eccentricities of the language in which we try to describe the world.'

Scientific Models

Mary Hesse

The conclusion that we have to deal with two sorts of scientific concepts, which we may call theoretical and experimental, leads us to look more closely at the actual function of the theoretical (or 'unobservable') concepts in theories. It suggests that we should try to describe theories in terms of two languages, as Ramsey did in his paper on logical constructionism. A description on these lines was worked out by N. R. Campbell in his book *Physics, the Elements,* over thirty years ago, and we shall take his example, the simple dynamical theory of gases, to explain how theories are actually used in modern physics.

The dynamical theory of gases was developed during the nineteenth century to expalin the behaviour of volumes of gas under pressure. Simple experiments, which are repeated by all beginners in physics, indicate that there is a relation between the volume in which a gas is contained, its temperature, and the pressure exerted upon it. Boyle's Law states that volume varies inversely as the pressure; Gay-Lussac's Law states that the absolute temperature varies directly as the pressure; so that the relation between the three quantities V, T, and P, can be written

$$P = c\frac{T}{V},$$

where c is a constant number. V, T and P are of course all operationally defined because they are directly measured. Now these laws can be regarded as first-order generalizations of the experimental results; they merely summarize those results in a convenient form, and the equation above is simply the mathematical expression for the curve which is obtained if the experimental results are plotted as points on a graph and the best-fitting and simplest curve drawn through them. But a scientific theory has to go further than this, and provide some means of linking this relation with other aspects of the behaviour of gases, with the chemical composition of the gases, their behaviour near the point of liquifaction, and so on. This is where second-order generalizations, or hypotheses, are required, and where concepts usually enter which are not operationally definable.

In the case we are considering it is postulated that gases consist of a large number of similar particles in random motion. The particles are called molecules because they can be shown to behave *as if* they were the same particles as those which have to be postulated in chemistry for different reasons, but we shall call them molecules for the moment without prejudging that conclusion. This hypothesis is expressed entirely in terms which can be dealt with by the simple theory of dynamics, and it is simplified still further by assuming that the molecules are so small that their diameter can be neglected, and perfectly elastic so that they do not lose energy when they collide with one another or with the walls of the vessel. It then involves only the number (n), mass (m), and velocity (v), of the molecules, but notice that there is no question at this point of being able to measure these quantities directly, for we cannot 'see' the molecules even under a powerful microscope, and our object is only to try to derive from this hypothesis as many of the properties of the gas as we can. In order to do this we work out in detail the dynamics of a system of such particles and see whether any of the relations arrived at can be identified with the laws of Boyle and Gay-Lussac by suitable identifications of the theoretical concepts n, m, and v, or combinations of these, with the experimental concepts V, T, and P. Such a set of identifications, which will be mathematical equations, constitute the *dictionary* which translates the theoretical language of the hypothesis into the experimental language of the laws. We find that it is possible to do this, if we relate the energy of the molecules with the absolute temperature of the gas, and make identifications of the total mass of the molecules with the mass of the gas, the pressure of the molecules impinging on the walls of the containing vessel with the pressure exerted by the gas, and so on. We also find that some of the theoretical concepts can now be operationally defined in terms of the quantities V, T, and P, but it is not possible to define in this way the 'number of molecules' or their 'mass'. These are theoretical concepts, and the absence of operational definition for them need not worry us. So far we have shown that the hypothesis satisfactorily explains the laws of Boyle and Gay-Lussac, but we do not know whether it is satisfactory as a scientific theory until it has related these laws to other aspects of the behaviour of gases. If it cannot do this it will only be a very complicated way of expressing these laws themselves, with the added disadvantage that it has introduced unobservable entities without any gain in scientific understanding.

The system of particles can be regarded as a dynamical *model,* or *analogue* of the gas. If a model is to be scientifically useful, it must be in itself familiar to us, with its laws well worked out, and it must be easy to extend and generalize it so that its other properties, which we have not so far used, may be related, if possible, with the other properties of gases. The model must have, as it were, a life of its own, which is independent of those properties of gases which we are using it to explain, and this is a much more essential requirement than that all its concepts should be operationally definable. This condition is satisfied in the case of a system of particles, because the properties of such systems are well worked out in the theory of dynamics. An obvious generalization of the model in this case is to take account of the finite size of the elastic particles and study the new gas laws derived from the more general hypothesis and dictionary. It is found that this does in fact lead to a law (Van der Waal's law) which is more accurate than that of Boyle, being applicable to more types of gas and over a wider range of volume and pressure. By other generalizations of the model, viscosity and thermal conductivity are introduced into the theory and with these additions it is possible to determine the values of n, m, and the quantity corresponding in the model to the diameter of the molecules. Each of these determinations adds to our confidence in the correctness of the theory and in the 'existence' of the gas molecules, which is now indicated by a large number of independent experiments. But, as Campbell points out, it is dangerous to assert 'There are molecules', without keeping in mind the nature of the inference to molecules. He says that the phrase 'There are molecules'

'. . . is a very useful and compact way of calling to our minds all the assertions and implications of the dynamical theory of gases. But it has this use only because we know all about that theory and are intimately familiar with it. To anyone not familiar with the theory it would not evoke the ideas which we associate with it; and such a person, in his endeavour to find some meaning for the phrase, would be almost certain to find a perfectly wrong meaning.'[2]

This sort of analysis of models can be carried out with most of the theories of modern physics. For instance the theory of heat conduction depends on the model of fluid flow; all wave theories and field theories depend ultimately on models taken from hydrodynamics, all atomic theories on models taken from classical mechanics.[3] Even the modern quantum theory, which seems to have departed very far from all classical conceptions, can be shown to depend essentially on the simple dynamics of particles – it makes use of analogies taken from this theory, but with restrictions of meaning. For instance Dirac's discussion of 'observables' arises from the fact that he is using the analogy of moving particles, which are assumed to have the usual properties of such systems – position, momentum, etc. – but some of these properties have to be restricted in meaning and are found to be related to each other in a complicated way when quantum phenomena are dealt with. Dirac's 'observables' are not observable in the sense of being operationally definable, but they are the quantities which *would be measurable if* we were concerned with a system of particles of a certain peculiar type, namely a system in which precise measurements cannot take place because of the crudity of the measuring instruments, and in which only the results of measurements are required to be taken into account. Evidence for the 'existence' of such systems of particles is of the same kind as evidence for the existence of gas molecules, but perhaps at present it is rather less strong, because the quantum theory is not as firmly established as the theory of gases.

Sometimes the models used in physics are purely mathematical in character, and this is why the word *analogue* is generally preferable to *model,* because the latter may seem to imply something mechanical or at least picturable. Most nineteenth-century scientific theories were mechanical, but this is no longer the case. For instance one of the analogues used in the general theory of relativity is non-Euclidean geometry. This is no less an analogue than the mechanical type of theory, for it satisfies all the requirements mentioned above of being a well-defined and well-worked-out theory which is known independently of the phenomena dealt with in relativity, and it contains within itself suggestions as to how it should be extended in the ways appropriate to theories of pure mathematics, by using the usual mathematical criteria of simplicity and generality. It is important to realize that these are the conditions for a good scientific analogue, not that it can be pictured in terms of a mechanical or any other sort of model, and mathematical analogues are less likely to tempt us in this way than mechanical ones. It is no accident either that mathematical generalizations like Riemann's geometry are often developed for their own intrinsic interest before an application is found for them in science. It is easier for the scientist to use one of the mathematical languages already available and well worked out than to invent a new one.

Dirac has this to say about scientific 'pictures', or what we have been calling 'analogues', and their use in atomic physics:

'In the case of atomic phenomena no picture can be expected to exist in the usual sense of the word "picture" by which is meant a model functioning essentially on classical lines. One may, however, extend the meaning of the word "picture" to include any *way of looking at the fundamental laws which makes their self-consistency obvious.* With this· extension, one may gradually acquire a picture of atomic phenomena by becoming familiar with the laws of the quantum theory.'[4]

Satisfactory analogies, however, do not only make the self-consistency of the theory obvious, but also give grounds for predictions and extensions of the theory.

Let us look for a moment at various ways in which analogy enters into science. Two extreme types of use can be indicated, and examples could be given at all stages between them.

First, there are minor and entirely heuristic uses, to suggest the next things to do, after which the analogy is discarded. Such analogies will obviously depend greatly on fortuitous circumstances and on the peculiarities of the investigator. Examples are necessarily difficult to find, because this type of analogy will not usually appear in the finished work. Some historical examples can be thought of — discoveries made 'by mistake' by the use of analogies afterwards found to be irrelevant, such as Kepler's model of the sun and planets as a wheel in which the sun as hub pushes round the planets on the spokes; or the way in which Hooke arrived at the force exerted on the earth by likening it to that on a particle whirled round at the end of a string. In such cases the method of discovery is unimportant, only the mathematical result, verifiable by experiment, appears in the final theory.

At the other extreme there are analogies which are implied in the whole way in which phenomena are observed and in the language in which theories are expressed. The particle theory has provided such an analogy ever since Democritus developed his philosophy of atomism. These analogies are sometimes generalized into interpretations of the whole universe, and there is often influence in the other direction too, for contemporary categories of thought and social conditions may take a hand in moulding the scientific analogies. For instance Wiener[5] suggests that there have been three stages in the scientific description of human beings according to what was the most typical machine in use during the period — first, in the seventeenth and eighteenth centuries, clockwork mechanisms described by analogies from dynamics; then in the nineteenth century, heat engines described by analogies from thermodynamics; and now communication devices described by analogies from electronics.[6] Analogies like these determine the phenomena to be taken into account, and therefore the direction of research, and the whole framework of a theory. They have enormous vested interests in a theory, and therefore they can never easily be abandoned when new facts do not appear to fit in with the system of explanation which the analogies presuppose. There is always the temptation to explain awkward facts away in order to save the basic analogies of a science, and this has happened in the history of science more than once, most notably with the analogy of mechanism. Perhaps it is still happening in other and more subtle ways.

If the philosophy of science is to be more than a purely formal analysis of the logic of science, we have to decide which of these types of analogy are the norm of scientific explanation. Should we deny that the fundamental analogies are essential to science, and thereby reduce all analogies to the level of aids to discovery, having in themselves no explanatory or descriptive value? Most logicians of science now maintain this view. Hutten[7] for instance describes the function of models in science in terms similar to the account given above, but he goes on to say that this usage of models never gives a reliable interpretation because they carry surplus meaning from crude attempts to understand the world and may therefore seriously impede the improvement of knowledge. He suggests that the 'semantic' rules, that is, the directions as to how the various concepts are to be combined in meaningful statements or equations, are contained implicitly in the model, but should be formulated explicitly so as to do away with the ambiguities of the model itself. But it is exactly this vague 'surplus meaning' which gives the clues for further development. It is easy to see now for instance what semantic rules are required for Maxwell's theory of radiation. Here the model of waves in a material aether implied too much — the analogy of wave motion was necessary, but not the implication of a material in which the waves travelled. But this could not possibly have been known until various calculations and observations had been made on the basis of obvious simple extensions of the original wave model. In other words explicit semantic rules, like all types of formalization, 'freeze' a theory at the stage at which it is formalized. Surely the heuristic function of analogies must be regarded as an essential part of scientific theories.

Why do logicians tend to apologize for the use of analogy and to depreciate those parts of scientific theory in which it is involved? In order to answer this we must look a little more closely at various meanings of the word 'analogy', as it has been used above, and as it is used in logic. In logic since the seventeenth century the word seems to have been restricted to mean identity of some of the characters of the things related by the analogy, so that, to take an example given by Francis Bacon, there is an analogy between teeth in animals and beaks in birds. The argument from analogy is based on the observation of characters which are possessed in common by two or more entities, and is supposed to justify an expectation that other characters will also be possessed in common. Thus if the analogues have properties $p_1, p_2, \ldots p_n$, in common, and some other properties different, we can argue to possession of another common property p_{n+1} with some degree of probability if the possession of $p_1, \ldots p_n$ is relevant to the possession of p_{n+1} but not otherwise. The difficulty is to make clear what is meant by one property being *relevant* to another. The moon and a cheese may both be round and white, but we cannot argue that therefore the moon would be good to eat. However the fact that shape and colour are not relevant to edibility, whereas for example smell might be, is itself derived from an analogical argument based on past experience of a correlation between smell and edibility. And so the attempt to define analogy in this way leads to a vicious circle, and in the last resort it seems as if the perception of an analogy is not reducible to a list of resemblances and differences, but involves an element of direct recognition of association of properties, and a valid argument from analogy must ultimately rest upon this recognition.

A similar difficulty arises with scientific theories which we have called 'analogues'. When it is said that a mathematical theory or physical model is an analogue, what is meant is that there are resemblances (usually resemblances of mathematical structure) between the theory and the phenomena being investigated. The resemblances are between certain equations deduced from the theory, and the observations. But to call these equations or the theory analogical, is to imply also that there are grounds for expecting that there will be other resemblances between equations in the theory and observations not yet made. It is these grounds for induction from past experience to future experience, or from particular observations to general laws, which remain obscure in modern logic. Mill[8] for instance, remarks that analogies can only be used as a guide in science − he says there is no argument from analogy unless his canons of induction are satisfied. But although Mill's canons describe the method used in an early stage in the development of a science − the stage of qualitative analysis of causes and effects − they do not fully describe the type of analogy we are dealing with in advanced mathematical physics, so that his discussion of the use of analogy is not relevant to our present problem. Keynes[9] enumerates the criteria of analogical argument in science in a way which is applicable to modern physical theories in his work on *Probability*. His criteria are in fact descriptions of the procedure of a scientist formulating a new generalization, namely to make it cover as many diverse types of phenomenon as possible, and to make crucial experiments to decide between incompatible generalizations which both describe the phenomena as observed to date. But this is only a superficial description of what the scientist does, and goes no way towards uncovering the assumptions which lead him to do it, or towards showing that prediction on the basis of theories thus produced is reasonable.

In modern logic then it would generally be agreed that an analogy in science means simply an identity of logical or mathematical structure between certain parts of a theory and the experimental results. The importance of the particle analogy in the dynamical theory of gases would then lie solely in the fact that the behaviour of Newtonian particles is in some respects identical with the behaviour of gases. When we have climbed to the abstract mathematics by means of the analogy we can throw the analogical ladder away. But this account does not seem to be adequate, because we have seen that purely formal theories having no analogy to anything are scientifically useless, they are merely complicated ways of expressing the experimental results. This fact suggests that the 'identity of logical structure' is an abstraction from a real analogical relation between the physical or mathematical model and the phenomena being investigated. Mere identity of some aspects of structure does not indicate why an analogy is useful in predicting future experience. There is no mystery on being able to abstract similar structures from diverse processes which have occurred in the past — given a sufficiently versatile mathematics it is generally possible to do that — but that is not a complete account of scientific analogies, which have also to provide grounds for prediction.

The philosophers to whom one most naturally turns for a discussion of the use of analogy are the medieval scholastics.[10] Their analysis depended, however, on an Aristotelian theory of substance and accidents which we have seen reason to reject in connection with modern physics, and so they can only help us indirectly. Nevertheless there is one point about their discussion of analogical predication which seems to have general validity, and which indicates that, in spite of a rather restricted metaphysics, they had greater insight into the analogical use of language than most philosophers from the seventeenth century until very recently, when there are again signs that some philosophers are prepared to take analogy seriously. The point is that the scholastic philosophers recognized three types of relation between the attributes of various subjects, whereas modern logic recognizes only two, namely identity and difference. To these two the scholastics added analogy, which for them is a basic concept, not reducible to identities and differences. Put in terms of their subject-attribute logic, this meant that qualities could be predicated of a subject in three ways: univocally, analogically and equivocally. For instance 'rabbit' is the name of a certain species of mammal which can sometimes be pointed out, or can be defined fairly precisely in biological terms. 'Rabbit' is therefore predicated univocally of every instance of this animal. To call a man a 'rabbit' is to use an analogical expression to describe a certain sort of human character. To call a certain type of cheese dish a 'Welsh rabbit' is to equivocate. This particular example of analogy is perhaps not a very good one, as the man in question could probably equally well be described in other ways not mentioning the word 'rabbit'. The analogy here has degenerated into metaphor. But the point about the scientific analogies we are considering is that they cannot be put into other and more precise terms without destroying their heuristic value — they are not reducible to identities and differences.

The distinction between metaphor and analogy can be illustrated by a better example. The word 'anger' is properly and univocally predicated of human beings. We may however speak of an 'angry sky'. Here there is generally no implication of a real similarity between the sky and a human being in a particular mood; we are using a metaphor, which could easily, but less poetically, be dispensed with by saying that we can see black clouds and hear a sound of thunder. But when we speak of an angry dog we are using something more like an analogy; we imply that the dog has a consciousness akin to, but not identical with, our own, and that something has annoyed him; in other words, there is a real similarity between human and canine anger which can be made the basis of predictions, for instance that if we switch off the radio he will stop barking. More significantly, we speak of an 'angry God', and here, at least for believers in a personal God, it becomes impossible to replace the predicate by any other collection of statements. We mean that God is angry as men are angry, and yet not as men are angry, because He is God and not man. It was the predication of human qualities of God that chiefly puzzled the medievals, for, although they recognized analogies within the finite world as well, they do not seem to have been very interested in them, possibly because they did not have to cope with anything comparable to our modern problem of the analogical use of language to describe unfamiliar structures in nature which are brought to light by experimental science.

We must perhaps go even further than the medievals. When we have to consider descriptions of nature in terms of mathematics, we must deny that mathematical structure is ever predicated univocally of natural phenomena. Mathematical structure is invented and rigorously defined within the confines of pure formal mathematics or logic, and to use it in the description of nature is never anything but analogical. For instance there is an analogy between the human brain and an electronic calculating machine, but this does not mean that their structures are identical. The mathematical structure has one sort of relation to the calculating machine, its use being hedged about with qualifications proper to electronics, and a quite different relation to the human brain, being even more drastically hedged about by qualifications about the behaviour and the nature of human persons. The mathematical pattern is not predicated univocally of machine and brain because they are in obvious ways different sorts of things, and the similarities cannot be simply abstracted from the differences, but only used analogically. On the other hand there is not complete equivocation, because the analogy gives useful pointers to the brain physiologist and the electronic engineer, and this, we are arguing, is evidence for a real analogical relation.

Philosophers of science seem to have swung during the last half-century from the extreme of regarding theories as univocal descriptions, in the belief in billiard-ball atoms for instance, to the other extreme of regarding them as pure equivocations. Perhaps we may hope that the new emphasis on language will encourage philosophers to take in hand the task of clarifying the use of analogy, in science and elsewhere, to describe real relations between things.

1. Reprinted from *Science and The Human Imagination* London: SMC Press 1954 pp. 134-146.

2. *Physics, The Elements*, p. 138.

3. Locke understood that the atomic theory is primarily analogical: 'We see animals are generated, nourished, and move; the loadstone draws iron; and the parts of a candle, successively melting, turn into flame, and give us both light and heat. These and like effects we see and know: but the causes that operate, and the manner they are produced in, we can only guess and probably conjecture. *Analogy* in these matters is the only help we have, and it is from that alone we draw all our grounds of probability. Thus observing that the bare rubbing of two bodies violently one upon another produces heat, and very often fire itself, we have reason to think, that what we call *heat* and *fire* consists in a violent agitation of the imperceptible minute parts of the burning matter. . . . A wary reasoning from analogy leads us often into the discovery of truths and useful productions, which would otherwise lie concealed.' (*Essay Concerning the Human Understanding*, IV, xvi, footnote 12.)

4. Dirac, *op. cit.*, p. 10.

5. Wiener, *Cybernetics*, p. 53.

6. See also *Doubt and Certainty in Science*, by J. Z. Young.

7. 'On Semantics and Physics,' *Proceedings of the Aristotelian Society*, 1948-9, p. 115.

8. *Logic*, pp. 253, 364, etc.

9. *Probability*, p. 222.

10. For discussion of their views see Mascall, *Existence and Analogy*, and Emmet, *op. cit.*, Chap. VIII.